10
MINUTE GUIDE TO

FREELANCE
GRAPHICS® FOR
WINDOWS® 95

by Michael O'Mara

A Division of Macmillan Computer Publishing
201 West 103rd St., Indianapolis, Indiana 46290 USA

Library of Congress Catalog Card Number: 95-71418

International Standard Book Number: 0-7897-0554-0

98 97 96 95   8 7 6 5 4 3 2 1

Interpretation of the printing code: the rightmost double-digit number is the year of the book's first printing; the rightmost single-digit number is the number of the book's printing. For example, a printing code of 95-1 shows that this copy of the book was printed during the first printing of the book in 1995.

Printed in the United States of America

Publisher Roland Elgey

Vice President and Publisher Marie Butler-Knight

Publishing Manager Barry Pruett

Editorial Services Director Elizabeth Keaffaber

Managing Editor Michael Cunningham

Acquisitions Coordinator Martha O'Sullivan

Product Development Specialist David Bradford

Production Editor Audra Gable

Designer Barbara Kordesh

Cover Designer Dan Armstrong

Production Team Claudia Bell, Anne Dickerson, Trey Frank, Jason Hand, Clint Lahnen, Bob LaRoche, Stephanie Layton, Erika Millen, Julie Quinn, Bobbi Satterfield, Scott Tullis, Christine Tyner, Karen Walsh, Kelly Warner, Jody York

Indexer Debra Myers

Special thanks to C. Herbert Feltner for ensuring the technical accuracy of this book.

CONTENTS

Introduction

The time has come. You have to prepare all the materials for a big presentation coming up next week. Creating all the charts, graphs, and bulleted lists is a formidable task in itself. In addition, you need an electronic screen show, 35mm slides, handouts for the audience, and notes for the speakers. Oh, and don't forget to make time for those last-minute changes. How will you get it all done?

You're going to need some powerful tools to get all that work done on time. Fortunately, you have the new Freelance Graphics for Windows 95 program. With Freelance Graphics, you can create all those presentation materials—and more.

What Is Freelance Graphics for Windows 95?

Freelance Graphics for Windows 95 is a powerful and sophisticated presentation graphics program. It's designed to make preparing high-quality presentation materials as quick and easy as possible.

Because it's designed specifically for preparing presentations, Freelance does a better job of creating the kinds of materials you need for a presentation than does a word processor, spreadsheet, or drawing program. Plus, Freelance creates the kind of output you need for your presentation. You can create 35mm slides, overheads, color prints, black & white prints, audience guides, and speaker notes, as well as screen shows complete with transition effects, sounds, and animation.

These Freelance Graphics features make creating a presentation even more efficient:

- *SmartMaster Looks* are templates that contain background treatment, colors, and formatting. Freelance automatically applies all of the elements of the SmartMaster you select to the entire presentation, which means all your pages have a consistent appearance—the hallmark of a professional presentation.

- *SmartStart content masters* give you a head start on creating a presentation by providing suggested presentation pages for typical presentations, ranging from a brainstorming session to a product positioning plan.

- *Charting* is easy in Freelance Graphics. You can enter chart data directly into the program, or you can copy and import data from your spreadsheet or other Windows programs. Then you can present the data using Freelance's rich selection of chart types.

- *Diagram Gallery* adds a professionally drawn diagram to your presentation. Just add text to make it your own. In addition, if you need to draw a custom diagram or flow chart, Freelance offers special tools (such as shapes with embedded text, and connecting lines that snap to the edges of shapes) to make the task easier.

Now your task is to learn to use this software to get your work done. You don't have time to plow through thick manuals or books that tell you everything you ever wanted to know about Freelance Graphics. You don't want to peruse Help files trying to find out how to perform simple tasks, and you certainly don't have time to waste using the "trial and error" approach.

WELCOME TO THE *10 MINUTE GUIDE* TO *FREELANCE GRAPHICS FOR WINDOWS 95*

Computer programs aren't always easy to wade through. There's a lot you need to know in order to make a program do what you want it to do. That's where this book helps. The *10 Minute Guide to Freelance Graphics for Windows 95* gives you straightforward, easy-to-understand lessons that teach you how to use Freelance to accomplish specific tasks. This book gives you the information you need, without all the technical jargon. And you'll be able to complete each lesson in 10 minutes or less.

The *10 Minute Guide to Freelance Graphics for Windows 95* is for anyone interested in:

- Fast and easy information about creating presentation graphics.

- Tips and steps for creating bulleted lists.

- Creating charts and diagrams.

- Learning about making a screen show of your presentation.

- Printing audience guides and speakers' guides.

How to Use This Book

Each of the lessons in this book includes step-by-step instructions for using the Freelance Graphics program. You can read the book from start to finish, or you can pick and choose the lessons focusing on the tasks you want to learn. The first few lessons cover such tasks as starting and exiting the Freelance Graphics program, getting to know the program, and getting help. Lesson-by-lesson, you progress to using Freelance to create bulleted lists, charts, and diagrams. You even find lessons about turning your presentation into a screen show.

Conventions Used in This Book

Throughout this book, you will see the following boxes. They provide additional information that you might need as you work through the lesson.

 Timesaver Tip icons mark tips that give you hints for using Freelance Graphics more efficiently.

Plain English icons identify definitions of terms you need to know to carry out the tasks.

Panic Button icons alert you to warnings and cautions about potential problem areas.

This book also uses the following conventions to help you distinguish important information:

What you type	Things that you have to type appear in bold, colored type.
Things you select	Keys that you need to press and items that you need to select appear in colored type.
On-screen text	On-screen messages from Freelance Graphics appear in bold type.

TRADEMARKS

All terms mentioned in this book that are known to be trademarks or service marks are listed below. In addition, terms suspected of being trademarks or service marks have been appropriately capitalized. Que Corporation cannot attest to the accuracy of this information. Use of a term in this book should not be regarded as affecting the validity of any trademark or service mark.

STARTING AND QUITTING FREELANCE GRAPHICS

In this lesson, you'll learn how to start Freelance Graphics, open a presentation, and quit the program when you're through.

STARTING FREELANCE GRAPHICS

After you install Freelance Graphics, you're ready to start the program and begin using it. Windows' Start menu is the most obvious way to launch a program. Unless you chose to override the standard installation settings, the Freelance Graphics setup program added Freelance Graphics to your Start menu. To run Freelance from the Start menu, follow these steps:

1. Click the Start button on the Windows taskbar.

2. On the Start menu, point to Programs.

3. When the cascading menu appears, point to Lotus SmartSuite. Another cascading menu appears.

4. Click Lotus Freelance Graphics 96 as shown in Figure 1.1. Windows starts the Freelance Graphics program.

> **Why Is It Different?** These instructions assume that you installed Freelance as part of the Lotus SmartSuite. If you installed the stand-alone version of Freelance, your menu items may be slightly different.

 If you have a shortcut icon for Freelance Graphics on your desktop, it provides an even faster way to start the program. To start Freelance Graphics from a shortcut icon, simply double-click on the Freelance Graphics 4.0 shortcut icon.

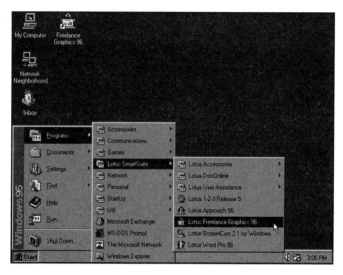

FIGURE 1.1   You'll find Lotus Freelance Graphics 96 on Windows 95's Start menu.

Shortcut Icons   If you don't have a shortcut icon for
Freelance Graphics, you can make one. Just open the My
Computer window or run Windows Explorer and open the
\Lotus\flg folder in which Freelance Graphics is installed.
Locate the main Freelance application file (F32MAIN.EXE),
drag it out of the folder, and drop it on the desktop. Win-
dows 95 creates a shortcut icon automatically.

Another way to start Freelance Graphics is to simply open a
Freelance presentation file. You can start from a file icon on your
desktop, on a floppy disk, or in a folder on your hard drive, and
you can use any of Windows 95's standard file management
features (such as the Windows Explorer or the My Computer
window) to open the file. When you open the file, Windows
recognizes that the presentation was created in Freelance
Graphics; therefore, it starts Freelance Graphics and opens
the presentation file.

Here are the specific steps for starting Freelance Graphics by open-ing a presentation file in Windows Explorer.

1. Run the Windows Explorer. (Click on the Start button, point to Programs, and click on Windows Explorer.)

2. Use the folder hierarchy in the left panel to open the folder containing your presentation file (see Figure 1.2).

3. Locate the presentation file in the right panel and double-click on it. Windows starts Freelance automatically and opens the presentation file. At that point, you're ready to view or edit the presentation.

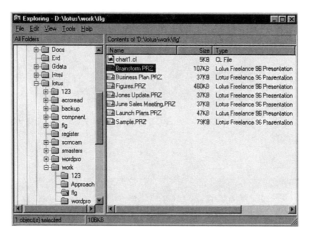

FIGURE 1.2   Double-click on a Freelance presentation file in Windows Explorer to quickly launch Freelance Graphics.

WELCOME TO FREELANCE GRAPHICS

If you start Freelance Graphics from the Start menu or a shortcut icon, you're greeted by the Welcome to Lotus Freelance Graphics dialog box shown in Figure 1.3.

TIP

Get Straight to Work   Starting Freelance by opening a presentation file skips the Welcome dialog box.

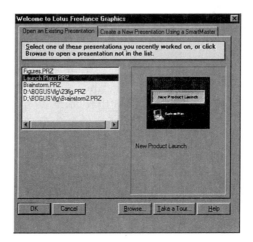

FIGURE 1.3   The Welcome dialog box greets you when you start the program.

That's Not the Screen I Have!   If you are opening Freelance Graphics for the first time, your screen will look slightly different. However, from now on, it will look like this one.

The options in the Welcome dialog box enable you to choose how you want to get started in Freelance Graphics.

- **Open an Existing Presentation**   Click on this tab at the top of the dialog box to see a list of presentations you've worked on recently. Select one of the presentation files from the list, and Freelance Graphics opens it for you.

- **Create a New Presentation Using a SmartMaster**
  Click on this tab to create a new presentation. This tab
  provides you with the same options that the New Presentation dialog box does (see Lesson 4).

 SmartMaster   A SmartMaster template controls the look
of your presentation. Each formatting template includes a
background, a border, a color palette, clip art, and preset
text formatting. Freelance applies the template you select
to each page in your presentation.

- **Take a Tour**   Click on this button to view a presentation containing an automated screen show that gives
  you a brief orientation to the features of Lotus Freelance
  Graphics 96.

Make your choice from the dialog box and click OK. Then have
fun looking around in Freelance Graphics.

QUITTING FREELANCE GRAPHICS

When you're ready to leave Freelance Graphics, you can use
either of two techniques to quit the program. Both are quick
and easy.

- Pull down the File menu and select Exit Freelance
  Graphics.

- Click on the Close button (the X at the right end of the
  Lotus Freelance Graphics 96 application title bar).

If you have any presentation files open, Freelance Graphics
prompts you to save them. Save any files you want to keep before
you exit the program.

In this lesson, you learned how to start Freelance Graphics and
how to close the program when you're finished. The next lesson
gets you acquainted with the Freelance Graphics screen and the
ways you can view your presentation.

2 GETTING TO KNOW FREELANCE

In this lesson, you'll learn about the Freelance Graphics window and the ways in which you can view your presentation.

START WITH THE CURRENT PAGE VIEW

When you start Freelance Graphics for the first time, one of the first things you need to do is learn where to find the tools Freelance places at your disposal.

Freelance offers three different views of your presentation: the Current Page, Page Sorter, and Outliner views. Figure 2.1 shows the default view: Current Page view. Current Page view displays your presentation one page at a time. You'll use this view when you do most of the detail work on individual pages of your presentation.

Although Figure 2.1 shows only one presentation window, you can have several presentations open at the same time in Freelance Graphics. Each open presentation appears in its own window, and you can choose any view for each individual window.

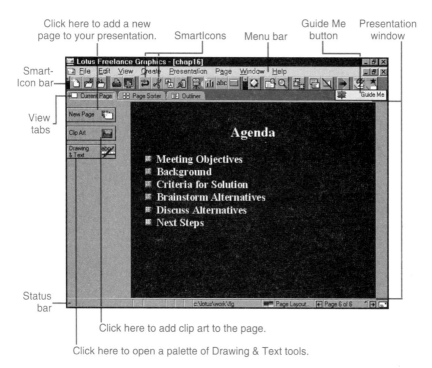

FIGURE 2.1 The Freelance Graphics window in Current Page view.

THE SMARTICONS

SmartIcons are buttons that provide one-click access to common commands and features. They're a convenient alternative to issuing commands with menu selections.

A SmartIcon bar such as the one shown in Figure 2.2 contains a group of SmartIcons. Freelance Graphics comes with several SmartIcon sets already defined and ready to use. Depending on what you're doing in Freelance, you may see more than one SmartIcon set at a time.

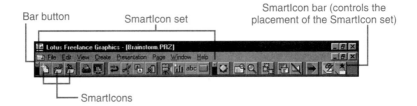

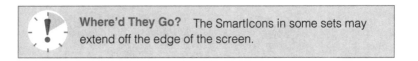

Bar button   SmartIcon set   SmartIcon bar (controls the
                                           placement of the SmartIcon set)

SmartIcons

FIGURE 2.2   Use SmartIcons to bypass the menu commands.

  Where'd They Go?   The SmartIcons in some sets may
extend off the edge of the screen.

A SmartIcon bar doesn't have to stay anchored across the top of
the Freelance Graphics window. You can move a SmartIcon bar to
either side or the bottom of the window, or you can position it as
a floating palette anywhere on the screen. Each SmartIcon bar
includes a tiny bar button in the upper-left corner that you use to
control that particular SmartIcon set. To move a SmartIcon bar,
follow these steps:

1. Point to the SmartIcon bar button (the thin bar at the left
   end or the top of the SmartIcon bar). The mouse pointer
   changes to a hand.

2. Drag the bar to its new location. The pointer changes to
   a fist as you drag. Release the mouse button to drop the
   SmartIcon set.

Which One Is It?   If you forget what a SmartIcon does,
simply point to it for a few seconds without clicking.
A cartoon-like bubble appears, giving the name of the
SmartIcon.

If you don't want to see SmartIcons, you can choose to hide an
individual SmartIcon set or all SmartIcons. To hide a SmartIcon
set, follow these steps:

1. Click on the SmartIcon set's bar button. Freelance Graphics displays a menu of commands you can use to control the SmartIcon set.

2. Choose Hide this bar of SmartIcons from the menu.

To hide all SmartIcon sets, open the View menu and choose Show SmartIcons. This command acts as a toggle switch; just repeat the command to make the SmartIcons visible again.

Not only do you control which SmartIcon sets Freelance Graphics displays, you can also control which SmartIcons appear in each SmartIcon set. Customizing SmartIcon sets is an advanced technique, but if you want to try it, pull down the File menu, choose User Setup, and then choose SmartIcons Setup. Freelance displays a dialog box in which you can change the contents of SmartIcon sets and even create new SmartIcon sets.

ZOOM IN FOR A CLOSER VIEW

Normally, Current Page view displays a full page that's reduced to fit within the workspace of the presentation window. If you need to take a closer look at some details on the page, you can use Freelance's Zoom In command to magnify the image. When you finish, you use the Zoom Out command to reduce the image.

- **Zoom In** Pull down the View menu and choose Zoom In to enlarge the page you're working on. (You can repeat the command to make the image larger and larger.) Use the scroll bars to bring different portions of the magnified page into view in the presentation window.

- **Zoom Out** Pull down the View menu and choose Zoom Out to reverse the effects of the Zoom In command one step at a time.

The View menu also includes three zoom commands that let you quickly switch to specific magnifications so you don't have to choose the Zoom In or Zoom Out command repeatedly. Experiment with the Last Zoom, Zoom to Full Page, and Zoom to Actual Size commands to see how they work.

PAGE SORTER VIEW

The Page Sorter view displays your presentation pages as a series
of thumbnail-sized images. This view enables you to change the
sequence of the pages in your presentation by dragging them into
a new order (see Lesson 10). You'll also use Page Sorter view to
create a screen show from a series of pages. Figure 2.3 shows a
presentation in Page Sorter view. To switch to Page Sorter view
from another view, pull down the View menu and choose Page
Sorter, or click on the Page Sorter tab.

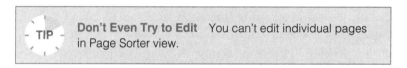

TIP   **Don't Even Try to Edit**   You can't edit individual pages
in Page Sorter view.

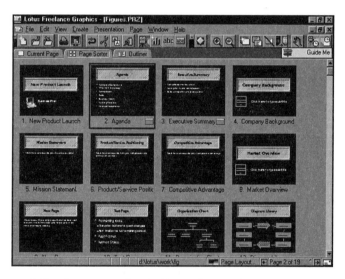

FIGURE 2.3   A presentation in Page Sorter view.

OUTLINER VIEW

Freelance's Outliner view displays your presentation as an outline. As you can see in Figure 2.4, this view even mimics the look of a yellow legal notepad. You can enter and edit text in Outliner view, which makes this view the easiest to use when working with the bulleted lists and text pages that are the mainstay of most presentations. You'll learn the details of using the Outliner view in Lessons 8 and 9.

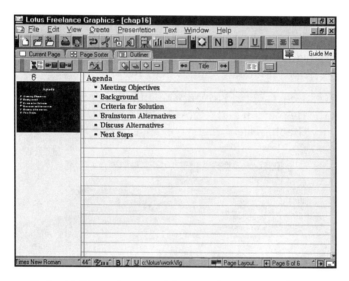

FIGURE 2.4   Outliner view provides another way to view your presentation.

To view your presentation as an outline, do one of the following:

- Pull down the View menu and choose Outliner.

- Click on the Outliner tab.

In this lesson, you learned about the major features of the Freelance Graphics window, SmartIcons and SmartIcon bars, and the ways you can view your presentation. The next lesson introduces you to the Freelance Graphics Help features.

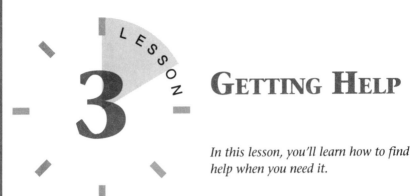

GETTING HELP

In this lesson, you'll learn how to find help when you need it.

FREELANCE GRAPHICS HELP

Freelance Graphics includes extensive online help. When you need to review a basic technique or see an explanation of a feature, help is just a few mouse clicks away.

To view a Help topic in Freelance Graphics' Help system, pull down the Help menu and choose Help Topics. The Help Topics: Freelance Graphics Help dialog box appears (see Figure 3.1).

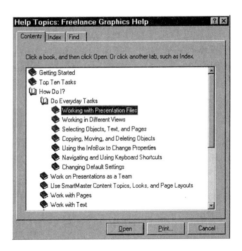

FIGURE 3.1 The Help Topics dialog box (with the Contents tab showing).

In this dialog box, you can search for the Help topic you're interested in. Three tabs offer you three different ways to search for a

Help topic. You'll see how to use each of the three tabs in just a moment.

When you select a Help topic and click on Display, the Help topic appears in its own window. As long as a Help topic window is open, it stays on top of Freelance Graphics and all other windows on your desktop. Even if you click on your Freelance Graphics window to continue working, the Help topic window remains visible so you can refer to it as you try the technique in Freelance.

SELECTING A HELP TOPIC FROM THE CONTENTS TAB

The Contents tab presents Help topics in a hierarchical structure similar to the table of contents of a book. The topics are grouped in categories and subcategories. If a book icon appears beside an item in the list, the item is a category that contains subcategories and/or Help topics. (An open book icon represents a category whose contents are currently displayed.) A page icon with a question mark in it appears beside each Help topic.

To select a Help topic from the Contents tab:

1. Pick a general category in which you think you might find the information you want. Double-click on the book icon to see the topics in that category.

2. If necessary, open any subcategories and scroll through the list to find the Help topic you're interested in.

3. Click on a Help topic in the list and click on the Display button.

SELECTING A HELP TOPIC FROM THE INDEX TAB

Just as the Contents tab is like a book's table of contents, the Index tab is like a book's index. The Index tab contains an alphabetical list of key words associated with the many Help topics (see Figure 3.2). You use it much as you would use the index of a book.

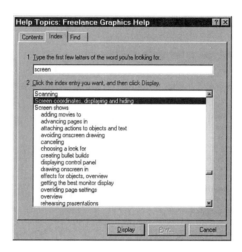

FIGURE 3.2   The Index tab of the Help Topics dialog box.

To select a Help topic using the Index tab:

1. In the first box, type the first few letters of the word you're looking for. The Help system jumps to that portion of the index list.

2. Scroll through the lower list, and when you find a likely index entry, click on it.

3. Click on the Display button, and Freelance Graphics displays the associated Help topic window.

SELECTING A HELP TOPIC FROM THE FIND TAB

The Find tab provides yet another way to locate a Help topic. It enables you to search the text of all Help topics for one or more key words you specify.

The first time you use the Find tab, Freelance runs the Find Setup Wizard to create a list of the words used in the Help topics. Just click Next and then Finish to have the wizard build the word list. When the wizard finishes its job, you see the Find tab (shown in Figure 3.3).

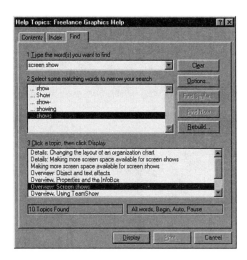

FIGURE 3.3 The Find tab enables you to search for specific words in Help topics.

To select a Help topic from the Find tab:

1. In the first text box, type the word or words you want to search for. In the second box, Freelance Graphics displays a list of related words.

Fine-Tune the Search Click on the Options button to open a dialog box in which you can control how the Help system handles the search.

2. Click on a word in the second box to narrow the search. Freelance conducts the search and displays the matching Help topics in the bottom list.

3. Click on a topic and click on Display. The associated Help topic window appears.

NAVIGATING A HELP TOPIC

No matter how you select a Help topic, you arrive at the same place: a Freelance Graphics Help window. Figure 3.4 shows you how to use the features in a typical Help topic window.

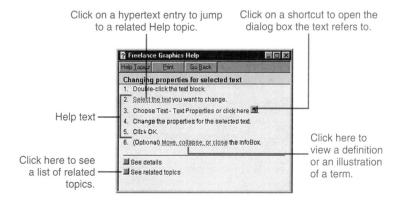

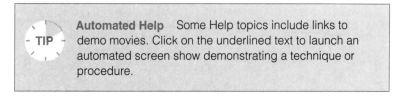

FIGURE 3.4   A typical Freelance Help topic window.

> ⏱ **TIP**   **Automated Help**   Some Help topics include links to demo movies. Click on the underlined text to launch an automated screen show demonstrating a technique or procedure.

If you want to search for another Help topic, click on the Help Topics button to reopen the Help Topics dialog box. When you finish viewing a Help topic, click the window's Close button (X) to close Freelance Graphics Help.

PRINTING A HELP TOPIC

Sometimes you'll want to print a Help topic for future reference. That's easy to do.

1. Click on the Print button.

2. Select (or confirm) the printer and the number of copies in the Print dialog box and click OK.

GUIDE ME BUTTON

Freelance's Guide Me feature gives you one more way to locate a pertinent Help topic. The Guide Me dialog box homes in on a Help topic by asking you a series of simple questions. You choose the answers from a list Freelance provides. Freelance adjusts the possible answers in the list based on what you were doing when you selected Guide Me.

To open the Guide Me dialog box (shown in Figure 3.5), do one of the following:

- Pull down the Help menu and choose Guide Me.

- Click on the Guide Me button in the upper-right corner of the presentation window.

Answer whatever questions Freelance asks. When Freelance has enough information to determine what you want to do, it displays the Help topic you need.

Click here to answer the question.

FIGURE 3.5   The Guide Me dialog box.

In this lesson, you learned how to access Freelance Graphics Help. In the next lesson, you'll learn how to start a new presentation.

CREATING A NEW PRESENTATION

In this lesson, you'll learn to start a new Freelance Graphics presentation and select its overall look.

In Freelance Graphics, you work with an entire presentation as a whole. You determine the look for your entire presentation, and Freelance takes care of applying that look consistently to all the pages in the presentation. Freelance automates the process with *SmartMasters*, presentation templates that contain background treatment and formatting information, and *SmartStarts*, suggested contents for common types of presentations.

Once you get started, you'll spend most of your time working with the individual pages of your presentation. However, you need to remember that each page is a part of the whole presentation. So before you can begin creating pages for your presentation, you have to start a new presentation in Freelance.

STARTING A NEW PRESENTATION

Freelance Graphics gives you two ways to start a new presentation:

- Click on the Create a New Presentation Using a SmartMaster tab in the Welcome to Lotus Freelance Graphics dialog box that appears when you start Freelance.

- In the Freelance Graphics window, pull down the File menu and choose New Presentation. Freelance displays the New Presentation dialog box shown in Figure 4.1.

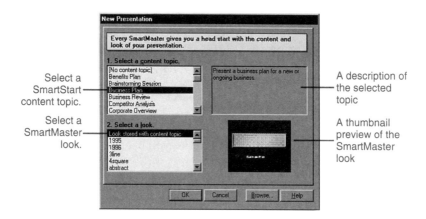

Select a SmartStart content topic.

A description of the selected topic

Select a SmartMaster look.

A thumbnail preview of the SmartMaster look

FIGURE 4.1   The New Presentation dialog box.

At this point, you have the same options whether you're working in the Welcome dialog box or the New Presentation dialog box.

SELECTING A TEMPLATE FOR YOUR PRESENTATION

You can create a presentation much more quickly and easily using a Freelance Graphics template than you can starting from scratch. Actually, Freelance relies quite heavily on templates: SmartStart templates control the content of a presentation, and SmartMaster templates control the look of a presentation.

SmartStart Content Master   A SmartStart template helps you develop the presentation's content. A SmartStart includes pages with suggested headings appropriate to that particular kind of presentation.

SmartMaster   A SmartMaster template controls the look of your presentation. Each formatting template includes a background, a border, a color palette, clip art, and preset text formatting. Freelance applies the selected template to each page in your presentation.

When you start your new presentation, you usually select a SmartStart and a SmartMaster template for the presentation. (If you really want to start off with a completely blank presentation, you can choose No Content and No Look. But most of the time, you'll want to take advantage of Freelance's templates.) You can change SmartMasters at any time. You can also change SmartStart templates by pulling down the Presentation menu, pointing to SmartMaster Content, and then clicking on Select a Topic. (You may need to click on Stop Using first to disable the current SmartStart.)

To choose the templates for your presentation, follow these steps:

1. Scroll through the Select a content topic list and select the SmartStart you think is most appropriate for your presentation.

No Exact Match   If none of the SmartStart templates seem to be exactly what you want, just use the closest thing. The SmartStart templates are only suggestions; you can ignore them or change the suggested pages as you develop your presentation.

2. When you pick a SmartStart content topic, it includes a SmartMaster. If you want to select a different Smart-Master, scroll through the Select a look list and pick a SmartMaster template for your presentation. To the right of the list, Freelance displays a *thumbnail* preview of the SmartMaster's look.

3. Click OK.

Thumbnail   A thumbnail is a miniature "sketch" of your presentation page. Freelance often displays these small thumbnails to let you visually identify pages or preview the effects of choices you make in dialog boxes.

CHOOSING A PAGE LAYOUT FOR THE FIRST PAGE

After you select the templates for your new presentation, Freelance automatically opens the New Page dialog box. By default, the title page of the SmartStart content topic is highlighted, and a thumbnail preview of the proposed page appears on the right side of the dialog box (see Figure 4.2).

FIGURE 4.2   The New Page dialog box automatically shows the title page of the selected SmartStart content page.

To choose a page layout for the new page, follow these steps:

1. Select a page layout from the list on the Content Pages tab or the Standard Page Layouts tab. (You'll learn more

about the options for creating new pages in Lesson 6. For now, just accept the page layout Freelance proposes.)

2. Click OK to create a new page using the selected layout.

Freelance opens a new presentation window and displays the first page of your presentation in Current Page view (as shown in Figure 4.3).

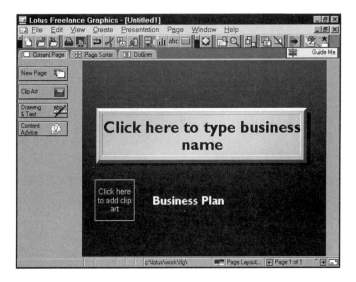

FIGURE **4.3**   The first page of your new presentation.

The page appears, complete with your chosen SmartMaster background and formatting. The "Click here" text serves a double purpose: it shows you a sample of the text formatting, and it provides content suggestions. "Click here" boxes make it easy to add clip art, charts, and so on, which you'll learn how to do in later lessons.

In this lesson, you learned to start a new presentation and select the templates on which you want to base it. In the next lesson, you'll learn how to save and update your presentation.

SAVING, CLOSING, AND OPENING A PRESENTATION

In this lesson you'll learn how to save a presentation, close a presentation window, and open an existing presentation.

UNDERSTANDING HOW FREELANCE STORES YOUR PRESENTATION

Before you save your presentation, you should understand something about the file you're creating. Freelance Graphics stores your entire presentation in one file: the Freelance presentation file. Therefore, in Freelance (unlike some other presentation programs), you don't have to create and keep track of a separate file for each page of a presentation. If you want to copy the presentation to a disk to transport it (to a conference, for example), all you normally have to have is that one file.

Although Freelance Graphics stores some bitmaps, pictures, and so on in the presentation file, it doesn't store all of them there. To conserve disk space, when you add an image to your presentation, you can choose to have Freelance store a reference, or *link*, to an image file that's located elsewhere on your system instead of adding a full copy of that image to your presentation.

 Don't Forget the Add-Ons   Normally, everything you need for your presentation is in one file. However, if you include linked graphics or special fonts in your presentation, you need to round up those files as well if you plan to copy or update your presentation.

SAVING THE PRESENTATION FOR THE FIRST TIME

To save your presentation in a file for the first time, follow these steps:

1. Open the File menu and choose Save As or click on the File Save SmartIcon. Freelance displays the Save As dialog box, shown in Figure 5.1.

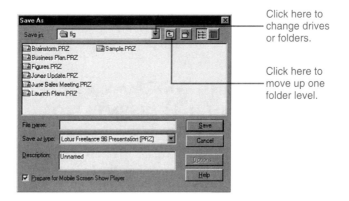

Click here to change drives or folders.

Click here to move up one folder level.

FIGURE 5.1 The Save As dialog box.

2. In the Save in box, select the folder in which you want to save the presentation file. If necessary, click on the drop-down list arrow or the Up One Level button to access other drives and folders.

3. Enter a name for your presentation in the File name box, using up to 255 characters, including spaces. Don't worry about adding a file name extension; Freelance does that automatically.

What Happened to My File Names?　Programs prior to Windows 95 are limited to eight-character file names and cannot handle these long names. If you think you'll need to use your presentation file with DOS or a pre-Windows 95 program, save the file with an eight-character file name. Although Windows 95 can translate long file names into eight-character versions for you, they can be pretty strange looking.

4. In the Save as type drop-down list, select Lotus Freelance 96 Presentation (PRZ) as the file type. (You won't use any of the other file types unless you need to send your presentation to someone using another version of Freelance or you want to export your presentation pages as image files for use in another program.) Freelance saves your presentation as the selected file type and adds the associated extension to the file name automatically.

5. (Optional) Type a short description of your presentation in the Description box.

6. Click on the Save button. Freelance saves your presentation to a file.

The Importance of the Extension　The file name extension tells Windows 95 which program a file was created in. As long as you don't change the extension Freelance adds to your file name, you can double-click on a presentation file in Windows Explorer or My Computer to open the presentation in Freelance.

UPDATING A PREVIOUSLY SAVED PRESENTATION

After you save a presentation the first time, subsequent saves are simpler. You don't have to deal with the Save As dialog box unless you want to change some of the settings.

To save changes you've made to a previously saved presentation, do one of the following:

- Open the File menu and choose Save.

 • Click on the Save the current file SmartIcon.

CLOSING A PRESENTATION WINDOW

As you learned in Lesson 1, quitting Freelance closes all presentation windows. But you might want to close a presentation file without quitting Freelance. You can close a presentation file in either of two ways:

- Open the File menu and choose Close.

- Click on the presentation window's Close button (the X in the window's title bar or at the right end of the menu bar).

OPENING AN EXISTING PRESENTATION

After you save and close a presentation, you may want to open it again. When you first start Freelance, one of your options is to open an existing presentation. To exercise that option, follow these steps:

1. In the Welcome dialog box, click on the Open an Existing Presentation tab.

2. Select the presentation you want to open from the list box on the left. A thumbnail preview of the first page of the presentation appears (see Figure 5.2).

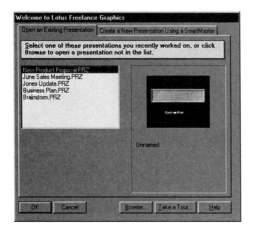

FIGURE 5.2   Select the existing presentation you want to open.

3. Click OK to open the selected presentation.

If you're already working in Freelance, follow these steps to open an existing presentation file:

1. Open the File menu and choose Open, or click on the Open an existing file SmartIcon, or press Ctrl+O. The Open dialog box (shown in Figure 5.3) appears.

2. In the Look in box, select the folder in which you stored your presentation.

3. Select the presentation file using one of these methods:

    • Click on the file icon in the file list.

    • Type the file name in the File name box.

    Freelance shows you a thumbnail preview of the selected file at the bottom of the dialog box.

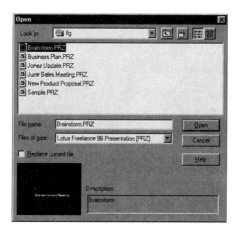

FIGURE 5.3   The Open dialog box.

4. Click on the Open button. Freelance opens the selected
   presentation, ready for you to edit.

Just Double-Click   You can also open an existing presentation file by double-clicking on its icon in a My Computer window, in Windows Explorer, or on your desktop.
When you double-click on the icon, Windows opens
Freelance and the presentation.

In this lesson, you learned how to save your presentation, close a
presentation window, and open an existing presentation. In the
next lesson, you'll learn about adding pages to your presentation.

Building Your Presentation by Adding Pages

In this lesson, you'll learn how to add pages to a presentation and how to specify the page layout for those pages.

Adding a New Page

In Lesson 4, you learned how to create the first page of a new presentation. However, most presentations consist of many pages, not just one. So you add pages to your presentation as needed.

Typically, you add pages to your presentation using the New Page dialog box. To do so, follow these steps:

1. Use one of the following methods to access the New Page dialog box:

   - In any view, open the Create menu and choose Create Page.

   - In any view, press F7.

   - In Current Page view, click on the New Page button.

   - In Current Page view or Page Sorter view, open the Page menu and choose New Page.

2. In the New Page dialog box, choose a page layout for your new page. (We'll explore the page layout options of the New Page dialog box in a moment.)

3. Click the OK button to create the page.

Freelance does offer ways other than the New Page dialog box to add pages to your presentation. You can add top-level headings from Outliner view, you can duplicate existing pages in your presentation, and you can copy pages from other presentations. We'll address each of these techniques in later lessons.

PAGE LAYOUTS AND SMARTSTARTS

Freelance's preconfigured page layouts make creating pages for your presentation fast and easy. Each page layout includes placeholders for text, charts, clip art, and other elements that are typical for presentation pages. The placeholders are positioned neatly on the page, and even the text formatting is taken care of. All you have to do is choose a "Click here" area and start entering your text or data.

When you create a new page, you can choose one of Freelance's standard page layouts. If you selected a SmartStart content topic for your presentation when you created it, you also have the option of selecting a content page. Content pages go one step further than standard page layouts by adding page titles and suggested text appropriate for a particular kind of presentation.

Of course, standard page layouts and content pages are just convenient starting points for your presentation pages. Once you create a page, you can use Freelance's tools to change it almost any way you like.

CHOOSING A STANDARD PAGE LAYOUT

If you chose not to use a SmartStart for your presentation, the New Page dialog box looks like the one in Figure 6.1. (If you are using a SmartStart, you'll find these same options on the Standard Page Layouts tab of the New Page dialog box.)

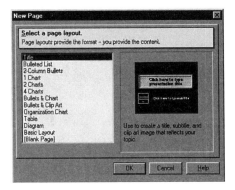

FIGURE 6.1   The New Page dialog box.

To select a standard page layout for your new page, simply click on the layout type in the list on the left. On the right, Freelance displays a thumbnail preview of the selected layout. Notice that the preview shows how the page will look with your presentation's SmartMaster look applied. Click OK to create a new page in your presentation using the selected layout.

TIP   **Build Your Own Layout**   If you don't find a page layout you like, you can create your own layout by adding text boxes, clip art, and so on to a blank page. Choose Basic Layout to work from a page that has only the basic SmartMaster elements in place. Choose [Blank Page] to work from a completely blank page with only a solid-color background.

CONTENT PAGES

If you chose a SmartStart when you created your presentation, your New Page dialog box looks like the one in Figure 6.2: it has tabs for Content Pages and Standard Page Layouts. Click on the Content Pages tab if it's not already displayed.

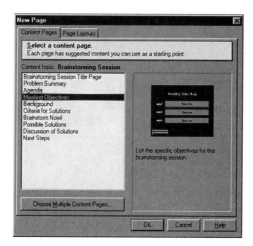

FIGURE 6.2   When you use a SmartStart, the Content Pages tab appears in the New Page dialog box.

The items in the list on the left will vary depending on which SmartStart you chose for your presentation. Selecting a content page is the same as selecting a standard layout. You click on an item in the list on the left, and a preview of that page appears on the right. Click OK to create the page.

Next, Please   Freelance keeps track of the last page of the SmartStart topic that you created. The next time you open the New Page dialog box, Freelance automatically advances the selection bar to the next content page in the list.

CREATING MULTIPLE CONTENT PAGES

If you use a SmartStart content topic, you can add multiple content pages to your presentation at once. You save a lot of time by not having to open the New Pages dialog box repeatedly and add pages one at a time.

To add multiple pages simultaneously, follow these steps:

1. Open the New Page dialog box (as described earlier in this lesson) and click on the Content Pages tab.

2. Click on the Choose Multiple Content Pages button to open the dialog box shown in Figure 6.3. Similar to the New Page dialog box, this dialog box also contains the list of content pages and the thumbnail preview. However, because you're adding multiple pages, you can select multiple content topics.

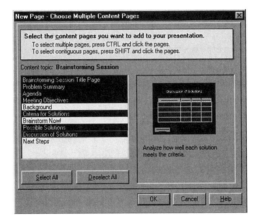

FIGURE 6.3   Add multiple pages to your presentation from this dialog box.

3. Select the content pages you want to create using one or both of the following methods:

   - Click on the Select All button to highlight all the items in the list.

   - Hold down the Ctrl key and click on individual items. You can select or deselect an item as many times as necessary without affecting the other selections.

4. When you finish making your selections, click OK. Freelance creates a new content page for each item you marked.

WHAT PAGE ARE YOU WORKING ON?

Once you've added several pages to your presentation, you need to be able to keep track of which page you're working on, and to move to other pages. Freelance displays the current page number in the status bar (see Figure 6.4); it appears in the form "Page x of x," where the first x represents the current page number and the second x represents the total number of pages in the presentation.

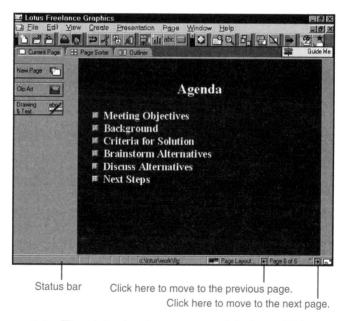

FIGURE 6.4   The status bar keeps you updated on which page you're on.

Freelance provides multiple ways for you to move around the presentation. To move to another page, use one of the following methods:

- Click on the arrows on either side of the page number (in the status bar) to move to the next or previous page in the presentation.

- Open the Page menu and choose the Next Page command or the Previous Page command to move to either of those pages.

- Open the Page menu and choose Go To Page. In the Go To Page dialog box (see Figure 6.5), select a page and click OK.

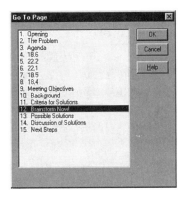

FIGURE 6.5   The Go To Page dialog box enables you to jump straight to any page in your presentation.

In addition to the techniques listed here, the Outliner and Page Sorter views offer more ways to move to different pages in your presentation. See Lessons 8 and 10 for more details.

In this lesson, you learned how to add pages to your presentation and select layouts for those pages. You also learned some ways to move to different pages in your presentation. In the next lesson, you'll learn how to enter text onto a page and create the most common type of presentation page: a bulleted list.

CREATING A BULLETED LIST

In this lesson, you'll learn how to create a bulleted list.

ENTERING BULLETED TEXT

A bulleted list is the most common page layout used in most presentations. As such, it's a good place to start when you're creating your first presentation pages. In Lesson 14, you'll learn to create text objects you can place anywhere on the page. In later lessons, you'll learn to create a variety of other kinds of pages.

To start this lesson, you'll need a new page to work on. Using what you learned in Lesson 6, create a new page in Current Page view. For the page layout, choose Bulleted List from the Standard Page Layouts. Your new page should look similar to the one shown in Figure 7.1. It shows the background you chose for your presentation and contains two "Click here" placeholders for text.

The "Click here" placeholders show you where this page layout reserves space for text. They also give you a preview of the formatting—the font, size, and color—the SmartMaster template assigns to that text. To create a bulleted list page using this page layout, you simply replace the placeholder text with your own text.

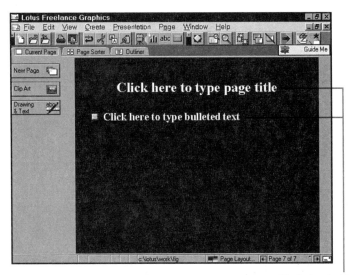

Text placeholders

FIGURE 7.1   A new page with the Bulleted List page layout.

To enter your title text, follow these steps:

1. Click on the Click here to type page title placeholder text. Freelance displays a text entry box. Figure 7.2 shows a text entry box; the blinking vertical bar insertion point indicates where the text you type will appear.

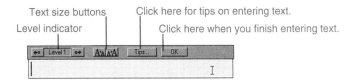

Text size buttons
Level indicator
Click here for tips on entering text.
Click here when you finish entering text.

FIGURE 7.2   The text entry box enables you to enter and edit text in Current Page view.

2. Type the title for your page. As you type, the text appears in the font, size, color, and alignment used by the active SmartMaster template.

Quick Edits   Use the arrow keys (or the mouse pointer) to move the insertion point; use the Backspace and Delete keys to delete text; use the Home and End keys to move the insertion point to the beginning or end of the text.

3. When you finish typing, click on the OK button to close the text entry box. The new title appears on the page, replacing the "Click here" placeholder (see Figure 7.3).

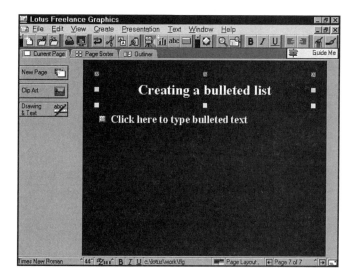

FIGURE 7.3   Your page title replaces the "Click here" placeholder.

Reopen the Text Entry Box   Double-click on the text to reopen the text entry box. You can reopen the text entry box and edit the text as often as you want.

CREATING BULLETS AND SUB-BULLETS

Entering text for a bulleted list is essentially the same as entering the title text. (You just enter more lines of text in the text entry box for a bulleted list.) The entire bulleted list goes in the same text box; you don't have to create a separate text box for each item in the list.

To enter text for a bulleted list, follow these steps:

1. Click on the Click here to type bulleted text placeholder text. Freelance opens the text entry box, with the first bullet already in place.

2. Type the text for the first item in the list. If you reach the right edge of the text entry box, just keep typing. Freelance automatically wraps the text down to the next line for you.

 Controlling Line Endings   If you don't like where the automatic word wrap breaks a long line, you can create your own line break by pressing Ctrl+Enter. (You can't press Enter to force a manual line break; that starts a new bulleted item.)

3. When you finish entering a bulleted item, press Enter to move to the next bullet in the list. The text entry box expands, and a new bullet appears.

4. Type the text for the next item.

5. Repeat steps 3 and 4 to add as many bullets as necessary to the list.

6. When you finish entering the bulleted list items, click OK to close the text entry box. The list appears on the page.

You're not restricted to using only one level of bullets in your list. You can indent some items to create outline-style sub-bullets up to five levels deep. The level indicator at the top of the text entry box tells you the bullet level of the selected item.

When you add an item to the list by pressing Enter, the new item starts out at the same level as the previous item. However, you can change indent levels before you type an item or at any time later using the methods described here.

- To create a sub-bullet, place the insertion point at the beginning of the line you want to indent and press Tab. Or, place the insertion point anywhere in the line you want to indent and click on the right arrow beside the level indicator at the top of the text entry box.

- To promote an item to a higher level (move it to the left in the display), press Shift+Tab or click on the left arrow beside the level indicator.

When you change the bullet level of the selected line, Freelance updates the level indicator, and the line takes on the formatting defined for the new level. Usually that formatting includes an indent and a different bullet (as shown in Figure 7.4). It may also include a different font or font size and other formatting details. (You'll learn to set the formatting for each text level in Lesson 15.)

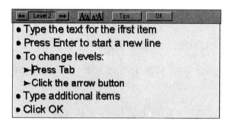

FIGURE 7.4 A bulleted list with indented sub-bullets.

REARRANGING ITEMS IN A BULLETED LIST

It seems like lists in presentations always need to be updated. Fortunately, Freelance makes it easy to add, delete, and rearrange items in a bulleted list. If you need to add, delete, or move items in a list, you simply reopen the text entry box and use normal text editing procedures to edit the list.

To add an item:

1. Place the insertion point at the end of the item after which you want to create a new item.

2. Press Enter to start a new line and type the text for the new item.

To delete an item:

1. Drag the pointer across the item you want to delete to highlight it.

2. Press Backspace (or Delete) to delete the text.

3. Press Backspace again to delete the bullet. Freelance adjusts the other items to fill in the empty space.

To move an item:

1. Point to the bullet for the item you want to move. The pointer changes to a hand.

2. Click and drag the bullet up or down the list. As you drag, the pointer changes to a fist, and a horizontal line indicates where the item will be inserted in the list.

3. When the horizontal line is in the desired location, release the mouse button to drop the item. Freelance moves the bulleted item and adjusts the others accordingly.

CHANGING BULLETS

Freelance adds bullets to a bulleted list automatically. You don't have to type codes or draw objects to create the bullets. In fact, Freelance treats a bullet as a formatting attribute of the text paragraph.

You'll get into formatting in more detail in Lesson 15, but right now let's take a quick look at how to change the appearance of the bullets. Although you can select an individual item in a bulleted list and change its bullet, more often you'll change the bullet style for all the bullets at that level in the entire list.

To change the bullets for a level, follow these steps:

1. Select the list by clicking once on the text, but do not open the text entry box. (Close the text entry box first if it's open.) Eight small squares called *handles* appear around the list.

2. Open the Text menu, choose Text Properties by Level, and then choose the level of the bullets you want to change (such as Level 2). Freelance opens the Properties for Level *X* dialog box.

3. Click on the bullets tab to see the options for bullets (shown in Figure 7.5).

FIGURE 7.5   This little dialog box contains the bullet formatting options.

4. Adjust the following settings to change the appearance of the bullets for this level:

> **Style**   Select the bullet style. You can choose from letters, numbers, and a variety of dots, boxes, and symbols. Choose None for no bullet, or choose Symbol to open another dialog box that contains clip art symbols you can use as bullets.
>
> **Color**   Pick a color for the bullets.
>
> **Size**   Specify the size, just as you would for text fonts.
>
> **Start Number**   Tell Freelance which number or letter you want your bullets to start with. For example, you can start with number 12 and count up from there. (This box is only effective if you choose a number or letter style.)
>
> **Bullet Shadow**   Use these settings to specify what kind of drop shadow you want to accent the bullet with. You can specify the Position, Depth, and Color for the shadow. If you don't want a shadow, select None in the Position box.
>
> **Space between bullet & text**   Tell Freelance how much space you want between the bullet and the text.

5. When you're satisfied with your settings, click on the Close (X) button to close the dialog box.

In this lesson, you learned to enter bulleted list text on a presentation page in Current Page view. In the next lesson, you'll learn about viewing your presentation as an outline.

LESSON 8

DISPLAYING YOUR PRESENTATION AS AN OUTLINE

In this lesson, you'll learn how to display your presentation as an outline, how to control the amount and kind of detail you see, and how to manipulate pages in Outliner view.

THE OUTLINER VIEW

Freelance's Outliner view lets you work with your Freelance presentation in outline form. An outline is a good tool for helping you organize your thoughts for a presentation, and it provides a good way to organize information for the presentation itself.

Outliner view is particularly appropriate for organizing the bulleted lists that are the backbone of most presentations. Each presentation page title appears as a major heading in the outline, subheads on the presentation page are indented one level in the outline, and bulleted items on the presentation page become bullet points in the outline. It's a natural extension of the way you probably work.

You can switch to Outliner view in either of two ways:

- Open the View menu and choose Outliner.
- Click on the Outliner tab in the presentation window.

Freelance displays your active presentation in Outliner view, as shown in Figure 8.1. Notice that the program even cleverly simulates the look of the yellow notepad that many people use for this purpose.

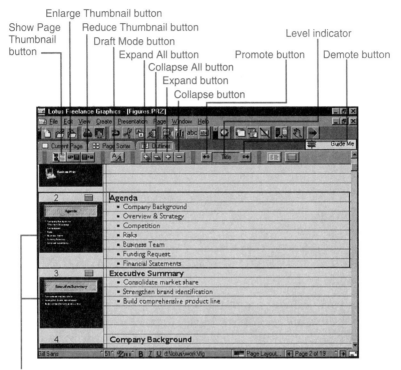

Enlarge Thumbnail button
Show Page
Thumbnail   Reduce Thumbnail button
button   Draft Mode button   Level indicator
              Expand All button   Promote button   Demote button
                Collapse All button
                  Expand button
                    Collapse button

Thumbnail pages

FIGURE 8.1   The Outliner view.

In Outliner view, you can work with text elements such as page titles and bulleted lists, without worrying about the graphical elements in your presentation. Although the charts, diagrams, clip art, and drawings show up on the thumbnail pages, you cannot work with them in Outliner view.

HOW MUCH DETAIL DO YOU WANT TO SEE?

Like the outliner feature in most word processors, Outliner view lets you expand and collapse the outline to control how much detail you see. You can collapse a page to show only the title, or expand it to show all the details.

To expand or collapse a single page, do one of the following:

- Open the View menu and choose Expand or Collapse.

 - Click on the Expand button (+) or the Collapse button (–).

To expand or collapse the entire presentation in one step, do one of the following:

- Open the View menu and choose Expand All or Collapse All.

 - Click on the Expand All button or the Collapse All button.

Showing or Hiding Page Thumbnails in Outliner View

Unlike your ordinary run-of-the-mill legal pad, Freelance can display a thumbnail image of each page beside the outline heading. You can choose whether you want to see the thumbnails, and you can select one of three sizes. If you choose not to display the thumbnails, Freelance displays a small page icon for each page.

Use either of these techniques to toggle the page thumbnail display on and off:

- Open the View menu and choose Show Pictures of Pages.

 - Click on the Show Page Thumbnails button.

When you have Show Page Thumbnails turned on, you can even choose the thumbnail size. To do so, open the View menu, choose Page Size, and then choose Small, Medium, or Large. If you prefer to use the buttons in the Outliner view, click on the Reduce Thumbnail button to make the thumbnails smaller or the Enlarge Thumbnail button to make them bigger.

Quick View Change   You can double-click on a page's thumbnail to open that page in Current Page view.

SIMPLIFYING THE DISPLAY WITH DRAFT MODE

By default, Freelance displays the text in Outliner view using the font and formatting it will have on the presentation page. However, sometimes it's easier to work with plain, unadorned text. For those times, you can switch to draft mode. To toggle draft mode on or off, click on the Draft Mode button, or pull down the View menu and choose Draft Mode.

SELECTING PAGES

To select a single page in Outliner view, you simply click on the page's thumbnail. Then you can copy, delete, or move the page. If you need to select more than one page, hold down the Shift key and click on additional adjacent thumbnails, or drag across the outline text for the pages you want to select.

 Selecting Multiple Pages   In order to select and manipulate multiple pages, the pages must be adjacent to each other.

REARRANGING PAGES IN OUTLINER VIEW

It's easy to rearrange the pages in your presentation when you're working in Outliner view. Just follow these steps:

1. Select the page (or pages) you want to move.

2. Drag the selected page up or down the outline list. A horizontal bar appears between page thumbnails (or page icons) to indicate the page's destination.

3. When the insertion point is where you want to place the page, release the mouse button. Freelance moves the page and renumbers the other pages in the presentation.

ADDING PAGES IN OUTLINER VIEW

One of the advantages of using the Outliner is the ease with which you can add pages to your presentation. In most cases, it's as simple as clicking the mouse pointer in the location where you want to add a page and then typing the page title. If you want to use the default page layout, that's all there is to it.

If you want to select a different page layout for the new page, click the Page Layout button at the bottom of the Freelance window and choose one of the standard layouts from the dialog box. If you're using a SmartStart content master, you can open the Create menu and choose Create Page, or right-click on a page thumbnail and choose New Page from the shortcut menu that appears. When Freelance displays the New Page dialog box, you create the page normally.

In this lesson, you learned how to display and work with your presentation in Outliner view. In the next lesson, you'll learn about the text handling features of the Outliner view.

WORKING WITH TEXT IN OUTLINER VIEW

9

In this lesson, you'll learn about the text handling capabilities available in Outliner view.

ADDING TEXT

The strength of the Outliner view is that it enables you to enter and manipulate text very quickly. For entering page titles and bulleted lists, the Outliner view is much more efficient than Current Page view. In the Outliner view, you benefit from being able to see the text on adjacent pages as you work. This makes it easy for you to see the flow of the presentation.

To add text to a page in Outliner view, follow these steps:

1. Click on a thumbnail to select the page to which you want to add text. The insertion point appears at the beginning of the first line—the title.

2. Type the page title and press Enter to start a new line. After the title, Freelance automatically indents subsequent lines to the next level.

3. Type the remaining text for the page, pressing Enter before each new item. You can type very long lines of text on the Outliner screen. Freelance automatically wraps long lines to fit within the text block on the presentation page.

The standard text editing techniques work in Outliner view. Click on text to move the insertion point to that location, or use the arrow keys to move the text cursor. As always, you can drag across text to select it, and then you can cut, copy, paste, or delete.

Format It   You can add text formatting using the Text menu commands and the status bar buttons. You'll learn more about text formatting in Lesson 16.

PROMOTING AND DEMOTING POINTS

A key feature of any outliner is the capability to promote and demote points easily.

Promote and Demote   To change the indent level of a line of text in the outline hierarchy. When you *promote* text, you move it up one level, making it more important; when you *demote* text, you move it down one level, making it less important.

To change the outline level of a line of text in Outliner view, follow these steps:

1. Place the insertion point anywhere in the line of text you want to change.

2. To promote the item, click on the Promote button or press Tab.

   To demote the item, click on the Demote button, or hold down the Shift key and press Tab.

Promote a Bullet to a Title   Promoting a line of text all the way to Title level transforms a subhead/bullet point into a page title. Freelance creates a new page for it automatically.

REARRANGING LIST ITEMS

It's easy to rearrange lines of text in Outliner view. And not only can you rearrange the bulleted list items within a page, you can also move items from page to page. The following steps tell you how to move a line of text.

1. If a page is selected, click on the text to deselect the page.

2. Select the item you want to move by clicking on its bullet (or in the blank space to the left of text where the bullet would be).

3. Click on the bullet, hold down the mouse button, and drag up or down the outline to the new location. As you drag, a horizontal bar indicates where the item will be inserted (see Figure 9.1).

This is where the selected text will go when you drop it.

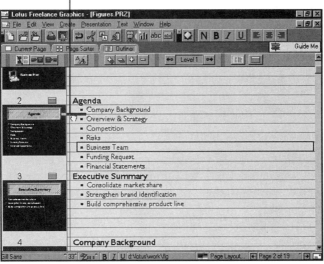

FIGURE 9.1   Rearranging text in Outliner view.

4. When the bar indicates the correct destination for the item, release the mouse button. Freelance drops the text in its new location.

BRINGING WORD PROCESSOR TEXT INTO AN OUTLINE

It's quite possible that some of the text you need for your presentation already exists in a word processor document. If so, you can move that text into Freelance instead of retyping it.

To transfer text from another document into a Freelance presentation, follow these steps:

1. Open the source document in your word processor program.

2. Select the text you want to transfer.

3. Open your word processor's Edit menu and choose Copy. The program places a copy of the text on the Windows Clipboard.

4. Open your Freelance presentation and switch to Outliner view.

5. Place the insertion point in the presentation where you want to add the new text.

6. Pull down the Edit menu and choose Paste. Freelance copies the text from the Clipboard into your presentation and creates new pages for the pasted text if necessary.

When you copy text from other programs, Freelance may be able to convert leading tabs into indent levels. However, most text is just pasted into your outline; you need to adjust the levels manually.

In this lesson, you learned to work with text in Outliner view. In the next lesson, you'll explore the Page Sorter view.

REARRANGING YOUR PRESENTATION IN PAGE SORTER VIEW

In this lesson, you'll learn how to use Freelance's Page Sorter view to delete, copy, and rearrange the pages in your presentation.

SELECTING AND USING THE PAGE SORTER VIEW

Freelance's Page Sorter view displays your presentation as rows of thumbnails (see Figure 10.1). In Page Sorter view, you can see many pages at once. Using this view to see how your presentation flows from page to page is like spreading printed pages out on a large work surface and stepping back to get a broad, all-encompassing view.

When you view your presentation as a whole in Page Sorter view, you shouldn't be concerned with the details on each page. Therefore, Freelance doesn't allow you to edit a page's contents in Page Sorter view. Instead, you use this view to copy, delete, and rearrange the pages of your presentation.

To switch to Page Sorter view, do one of the following:

- Click on the Page Sorter tab in the presentation window.

- Open the View menu and choose Page Sorter.

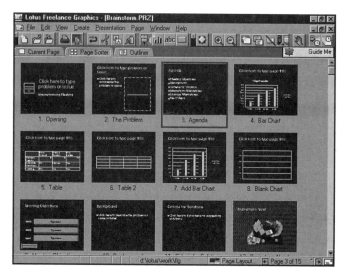

FIGURE 10.1   The Page Sorter view.

MOVING TO A DIFFERENT PAGE IN A PRESENTATION

You can use Page Sorter view as a visual index to your presentation. It's often the fastest way to locate a particular page in your presentation. If you need to do that, you can switch to Page Sorter view from anywhere in the presentation. When you locate the correct page, you simply click on the page thumbnail and switch to another view. The selected page is displayed.

TIP   **Find and Edit**   Use Page Sorter view to quickly find the page you want to edit. Select the page, and then switch to another view to make changes to the page.

You can use either of these shortcuts to access one of the other views from the Page Sorter view.

- Click on a thumbnail to select the page, and then switch to Outliner view or Current Page view.

- Double-click on a thumbnail. Freelance immediately displays the selected page in Current Page view.

MANIPULATING PAGES

Suppose you just finished creating a presentation, and you've switched to Page Sorter view to see how it looks. If you're not quite satisfied with the overall presentation, you don't have to start over. In Freelance, you can add, delete, rearrange, copy, and rename the pages in your presentation. While you can perform these tasks in any view, you can perform them more quickly and easily in Page Sorter view.

ADDING A PAGE

To add a page to your presentation in Page Sorter view, follow these steps:

1. Select the page you want the new page to follow.

2. Open the Page menu and choose New Page.

3. In the New Page dialog box, pick a page layout or content page and click OK.

DELETING A PAGE

The following steps teach you how to delete a page from your presentation:

1. Click on the thumbnail page you want to delete. A black border outlines the thumbnail to indicate that it is selected.

2. Open the Page menu and choose Delete Page. Freelance deletes the page, closes up the blank space in the Page Sorter display, and renumbers the remaining pages.

TIP **Quick Page Delete** In Page Sorter view, you can quickly delete a page by selecting its thumbnail and pressing the Delete key.

REARRANGING PAGES

To move pages around within your presentation, follow these steps:

1. Select the page you want to move.

2. Press and hold down the left mouse button. The pointer changes to a hand, and a dotted outline appears around the selected thumbnail as you drag the page toward its new location.

3. Position the hand pointer in the space between two pages where you want to insert the page you're moving. A gray vertical bar appears at the insertion point.

4. Release the mouse button to drop the page. Freelance moves the page to its new location, rearranges the display to close up any extra space, and renumbers the pages in their new sequence.

COPYING PAGES

To make a copy of a page in your presentation, follow these steps:

1. Select the page you want to copy.

2. Open the Page menu and choose Duplicate Page. Freelance makes a copy of the selected page and adds it to your presentation immediately after the original page.

3. Move the copied page to wherever you want it.

You Don't Want an Exact Copy?   If you want to use a
page very similar to one you've already created, first
make a copy of the existing page. Then double-click on it
to access Current Page view, where you can make any
necessary changes. When you finish, you can switch
back to Page Sorter view and rename the page.

RENAMING PAGES

The page name appears below the thumbnail page in Page Sorter
view and in a few other places in Freelance as well. By default,
Freelance uses a page's page number as the page name. To change
a page name, follow these steps:

1. Right-click on a thumbnail page and choose Page Properties from the shortcut menu that appears. Freelance
   displays the Properties for Page dialog box shown in
   Figure 10.2.

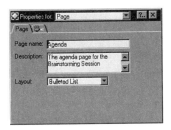

FIGURE 10.2   Renaming a page.

2. Type a new name in the Page name box. While you're
   here, you may want to change the description as well.

3. Click on the Close (X) button to close the dialog box,
   and Freelance updates the page name in the presentation
   window.

COPYING PAGES FROM ANOTHER PRESENTATION

One of the great things about Freelance is the ease with which you can reuse pages from other presentations. Freelance's Presentation Browser is designed to give you quick access to another presentation and to facilitate the copying of those pages into your current presentation. When you do this, the copied pages take on the look of your current presentation (they pick up the look from your presentation's SmartMaster).

To copy pages from another presentation file, follow these steps:

1. Pull down the Page menu and choose Copy Pages from Other Files. The Presentation Browser appears (see Figure 10.3).

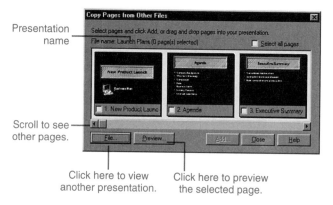

Presentation name —

Scroll to see other pages —

Click here to view another presentation.   Click here to preview the selected page.

FIGURE 10.3   The Presentation Browser.

The Select Presentation Dialog Box   If this is the first time you've used the Presentation Browser in this Freelance session, the Select Presentation dialog box appears automatically. It is essentially the same as the Open dialog box: you use it to select the presentation from which you want to copy pages.

2. If you've used the Presentation Browser before, it automatically displays the last presentation you viewed. If you want to open a presentation other than the one currently displayed, click on the File button and select the presentation file from the dialog box that appears.

3. To copy *one* page from the Presentation Browser, simply drag the thumbnail page from the Presentation Browser and drop it into your presentation. When you start to drag the thumbnail page, Presentation Browser disappears so you can see your presentation. Presentation Browser reappears as soon as you drop the copied page.

   To copy *multiple* pages from the Presentation Browser, mark each page you want to copy by clicking on the check box in the lower-left corner of its thumbnail. Then click the Add button. Freelance opens a small dialog box that lets you specify whether you want to add the pages before or after the current page or at the end of the presentation. When you make your selection, Freelance copies the marked pages and inserts them into your presentation.

 TIP **Copy Them All** Check the Select all pages check box to select all the pages in the Presentation Browser and copy them to your current presentation.

4. When you finish using the Presentation Browser, click the Close (X) button. Back in your presentation in Page Sorter view, manipulate the pages you copied as necessary.

In this lesson, you learned to manipulate your presentation in Page Sorter view. In the next lesson, you'll learn how to change the look of your presentation by changing page layouts, the SmartMaster, and the background.

CHANGING THE LOOK OF YOUR PRESENTATION

In this lesson, you'll learn how to change the look of your presentation by changing the SmartMaster, the background, and the page layout.

CHANGING THE SMARTMASTER

Much of the look of your presentation and its pages is determined by the SmartMaster template. The SmartMaster includes the background treatment, color scheme, and text formatting, among other things. As you learned in Lesson 4, you select a SmartMaster when you start a presentation.

The SmartMaster serves as the basis for every page in your presentation. This gives your presentation a uniform look. It also makes it easy to change that look by changing the presentation's SmartMaster.

Follow these steps to change the SmartMaster for a presentation:

1. Open the Presentation menu and choose the Choose a Different SmartMaster Look command. Freelance opens the Choose a Look for Your Presentation dialog box, shown in Figure 11.1.

2. Pick a new SmartMaster by selecting its name from the list box, or by using the arrow and scan buttons to display the desired SmartMaster in the thumbnail preview.

3. Click OK. Freelance closes the dialog box and applies the new SmartMaster to your presentation, changing the background, color scheme, and other SmartMaster properties on every page.

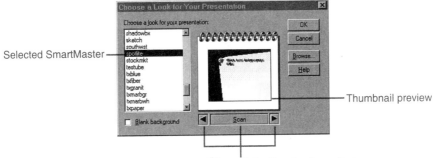

Selected SmartMaster

Thumbnail preview

Use these buttons to scroll through the thumbnail previews.

FIGURE 11.1   The Choose a Look for Your Presentation dialog box.

CHANGING THE BACKGROUND

Sometimes you don't want to change the whole SmartMaster for a presentation, you just want to change the background (or presentation backdrop). To change the page background, follow these steps:

1. Open the Presentation menu and choose Edit Backdrop. Freelance switches to the Current Layout view where you can edit the SmartMaster presentation backdrop (see Figure 11.2).

2. Right-click on the background to open the shortcut menu, and then choose Backdrop Properties. The Properties for Page dialog box appears.

3. Select a new pattern and colors for the background, and then click the Close (X) button to close the dialog box.

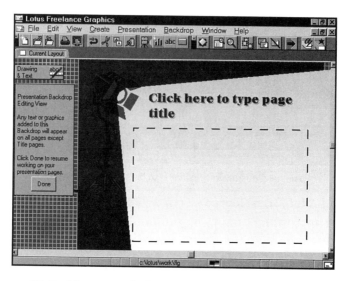

Figure 11.2   You can edit the presentation backdrop.

4. While you have the backdrop open, you can make other changes (move and edit objects, draw new objects, or add a logo, for example). When the background looks the way you want it to, click on the Done button in the lower-left corner. Freelance switches back to the previous view of your presentation and displays your pages with the new background.

Because the background color and the other elements of the presentation backdrop are part of the SmartMaster, any changes you make to the backdrop will affect all the pages in your presentation.

MANUALLY CHANGING A PAGE LAYOUT

As you learned in Lesson 6, you can assign a page layout (an arrangement of basic elements such as charts and text blocks) to a presentation page when you create it. But you're not stuck with that page layout forever. You can change it easily.

One way to change the page layout of a single page is to simply move the elements around. You can select a block of text or a clip art picture, for example, and move it, resize it, or delete it. You'll learn how to select and manipulate objects in Lesson 12.

 But I Don't Want to Change Them All!   If you want to rearrange one page's layout manually, and you don't want subsequent changes you make to the underlying layout to undo your work, you need to break the link between this page and the standard page layout. To do so, open the Page menu and choose Unlink Page Layout.

SELECTING A NEW STANDARD PAGE LAYOUT

Another way to change the page layout for a given page is to select a different standard page layout. For instance, if you want to add a chart to a page that uses the Bulleted List page layout, you can switch to the Bullets and Chart page layout.

To switch page layouts for a given page, follow these steps:

1. Click on the Page Layout button on the status bar, or open the Page menu and choose Switch Page Layout. Either way, Freelance displays the Switch Page Layout dialog box.

2. Select a new page layout from the dialog box.

3. Click OK, and Freelance applies the new page layout to the page.

The New Page Layout Didn't Take   When Freelance applies the new page layout to the current page, it automatically moves, resizes, and adds elements as necessary. However, it won't delete an element such as clip art that already exists on the page to make room for a new element that goes in the same location. To avoid the problem, delete such elements before you change the page layout.

Modifying a Standard Page Layout

If the standard page layout that's applied to a page doesn't fit your needs, you can rearrange things on the page manually. However, if you have a number of pages with the same page layout, you don't want to repeat those changes on each one. Fortunately, Freelance maintains a link between the underlying page layout and all the pages based on it. This enables you to make the change to one page and let Freelance take care of applying it to all the affected pages.

To modify a standard page layout, follow these steps:

1. Open the Presentation menu and choose Edit Page Layouts. The Edit Page Layout dialog box appears (see Figure 11.3).

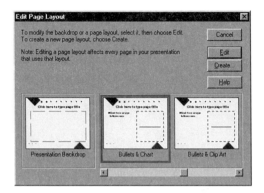

FIGURE 11.3 The Edit Page Layout dialog box.

2. Select the layout you want to modify (the page layout for the current page is highlighted by default). Then click on the Edit button. Freelance displays the selected page layout in Current Layout view.

3. Make your changes to the page layout. For instance, you might swap the positions of the clip art and the bulleted list. (See the next lesson for instructions on selecting and moving objects.)

4. Click Done to record the changes to the page layout. Freelance switches back to your presentation view and applies the changes to all the pages in your presentation that are based on that particular page layout.

In this lesson, you learned how to change the look of your presentation by changing the SmartMaster, background, and page layout. In the next lesson, you'll learn how to select and manipulate objects.

12

SELECTING AND WORKING WITH OBJECTS

In this lesson, you'll learn how to select objects in different ways and how to copy, move, resize and delete objects.

SELECTING OBJECTS

Freelance treats every element on a page—a block of text, a chart, or a clip-art picture, for example—as an object or unit. You can select and manipulate any object to make the page look the way you want.

 When an Object Isn't an Object In some cases, what seems to be an object (such as a chart) is really a group of several smaller objects (such as the bars and axis lines of a chart) that are locked together. You'll learn about groups in Lesson 24. For now, you can ignore the distinction between individual objects and groups that you select and manipulate as objects.

In general, you must select an object before you can do anything with it. If you want to edit text, you must first tell Freelance which text you want to edit by selecting the text block. Similarly, you must select other kinds of objects before you can move, resize, copy, or delete them.

When you select an object in the Current Page view, small squares or corners called *handles* appear around the selected object. Figure 12.1 shows a clip-art object and a polygon shape selected. The handles identify the selected objects and enable you to manipulate them.

Selected object   Handles

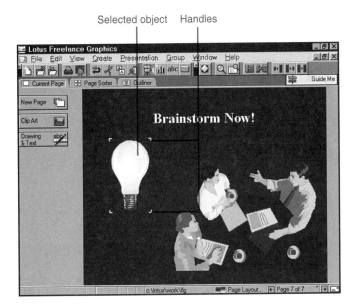

FIGURE 12.1   Handles mark a selected object.

The next three sections teach you different ways of selecting objects.

CLICKING ON AN OBJECT

The most straightforward way to select an object is to simply click on it. To select a different object, just click on the new object; Freelance automatically deselects any previously selected objects.

If you need to select more than one object, press the Shift key and click on each one. This selects the new object without deselecting previously selected ones.

Shift+Click to Deselect   You can Shift+click on a selected object to deselect it without changing the status of other selected objects on the page. This comes in handy when you're selecting several objects and you accidentally select one wrong object.

TIP

CYCLING THROUGH OBJECTS

Sometimes you can't just click on the object you want to select because it's inaccessible (hidden behind another object). If you can't get to an object to click on it, you can tell Freelance to highlight each object on the page in succession. When the object you want is highlighted, you can select it.

Follow these steps to tell Freelance to cycle through the objects.

1. Open the Edit menu, choose Select, and then choose Cycle to open the Cycle Selection dialog box shown in Figure 12.2.

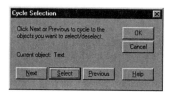

FIGURE 12.2   The Cycle Selection dialog box.

2. Click on the Next button or the Previous button to have Freelance highlight the next object in the specified direction.

3. When the object you want to select is highlighted, click the Select button. (If the highlighted object is already selected, you see a Deselect button instead of a Select button; click Deselect to deselect the object.)

4. When you want to quit cycling through the objects, click OK to close the dialog box.

Select Everything   You can select everything on the page at once. Open the Edit menu, choose Select, and choose All. Freelance selects all the objects on the page (but not objects on the SmartMaster background).

TIP

Clear the Selections To clear all selections, open the
Edit menu, choose Select, and then choose None.
Freelance deselects all selected objects.

SELECTING LIKE OBJECTS

If you have a number of similar objects on a page, you can select
one object and then have Freelance find and select all the other
objects like it. This is handy when you need to select all the yellow text or all the blue rectangles with black borders.

To select like objects follow these steps:

1. Highlight one example of the type of object you want to
   select.

2. Open the Edit menu, choose Select, and choose Like
   to open the Select Like Objects dialog box (shown in
   Figure 12.3).

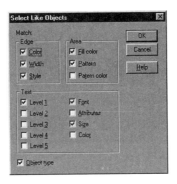

FIGURE 12.3 The Select Like Objects dialog box.

3. Choose the object attributes that you want to match and
   click OK. Freelance compares all the objects on the page
   to the original selected object and selects all those that
   match the criteria you specified in the dialog box.

COPYING AN OBJECT

Once you select an object (or objects), you can make a copy of it. You can make copies using the Copy command and the Windows Clipboard, or you can make instant copies with Freelance's Replicate command.

To copy an object using the Clipboard, follow these steps:

1. Select the object (or objects) you want to copy.

2. Open the Edit menu and choose Copy (or press Ctrl+C) to copy the object to the Windows Clipboard.

3. Move to a different presentation or page if necessary, and click in the location where you want to place the copy.

4. Open the Edit menu and choose Paste (or press Ctrl+V) to paste the object from the Clipboard onto the current page.

To duplicate an object on the same page, follow these steps:

1. Select the object you want to copy.

2. Pull down the Edit menu and choose Replicate (or press Ctrl+F3). Freelance makes a copy of the selected object and places it on the page, slightly offset from its original location.

After you use the Replicate command, you can use the techniques in the next section to move the copied object.

MOVING AN OBJECT

After you select an object, moving it is quick and easy. Simply follow these steps to move an object:

1. Select the object you want to move.

2. Click on that object (not on the background or another object within the selection handles) and drag. When you

start to drag, the pointer changes to a fist. A dotted rectangle moves with the fist to represent the object's location (see Figure 12.4).

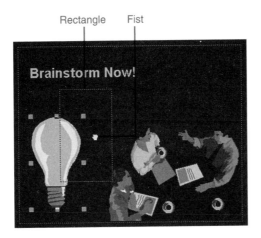

Rectangle   Fist

Brainstorm Now!

FIGURE 12.4   Moving an object.

3. When the rectangle is where you want the object to be, release the mouse button to drop the object. Freelance moves the object to the new location.

RESIZING AN OBJECT

The selection handles do more than just mark an object as selected. They also enable you to resize the object. To resize an object, follow these steps:

1. Select the object you want to resize.

2. Point at one of the object's selection handles. The pointer changes to a two-headed arrow.

3. Drag the handle to resize the object. Dragging a handle away from the center of the object stretches the object and makes it larger. Dragging a handle toward the center of the object makes the object smaller. As you drag, a dotted rectangle represents the object's new size.

4. When the rectangle appears to be the size you want, release the mouse button. Freelance resizes the object accordingly.

Controlling Distortion   To avoid distorting the shape of an object as you resize it, hold down the Shift key and drag one of the object's corner handles. Freelance keeps the height and width proportions consistent as you resize the object.

DELETING AN OBJECT

Deleting an object is perhaps the simplest form of object manipulation. To delete an object from the page, follow these steps:

1. Select the object you want to delete.

2. Open the Edit menu and choose Clear (or just press the Delete key). Freelance deletes the object from the page.

Oops, I Didn't Mean to Delete That   If you make a mistake and delete the wrong object, open the Edit menu and choose Undo. Freelance reverses your last action, restoring the object to the page. By repeating the command, you can step back through your last several actions.

In this lesson, you learned how to select objects and how to copy, move, resize, and delete the objects you select. In the next lesson, you'll learn to work with colors and color schemes.

WORKING WITH COLORS

In this lesson, you'll learn how to specify colors for the objects on your Freelance presentation pages.

UNDERSTANDING COLOR CHOICES

Color is an important part of most presentations, and choosing colors is an important part of creating your presentation pages. Freelance has a powerful color feature, but it keeps color selection simple by providing color palettes that are tied to SmartMasters.

Freelance's color palettes can contain any of several million possible colors. You can use a *color library* of up to 256 colors—which is usually more than enough—in a Freelance presentation. You can even custom blend colors and add them to the library. (The default Freelance color library includes 240 standard colors plus 16 spaces for custom colors; however, you can redefine any color in the library if necessary.)

SMARTMASTER COLORS VS. STATIC COLORS

Every SmartMaster template includes a *color palette*, a subset of colors from the color library, that the SmartMaster designer chose to go together. By default, all of the objects in your presentation use colors from the color palette of the SmartMaster you're using. When you change SmartMasters in a presentation, you change color palettes as well. As a result, all the objects (title text, background, chart lines, and so on) that were assigned colors from the original SmartMaster's color palette change color automatically.

When you create and color objects of your own, you can choose their colors from the color palette associated with your

SmartMaster. If you do, those objects also change color when you change SmartMasters. Therefore, you should use the SmartMaster colors so you always know the colors of your own objects will coordinate with the colors of any SmartMaster you decide to use.

Suppose, however, that you want to create a company logo or some other object and you don't want its color to change. When you want to assign a *static color* to an object, simply choose your color from the large color library instead of from the SmartMaster color palette. When you assign a color that's not from a Smart-Master palette, changing the SmartMaster has no effect on the color of the object.

Static Color   Any color that's not on the SmartMaster color palette. Static colors do not change when you change to a different SmartMaster for your presentation.

Selecting a Color with a Color Chooser

When you need to specify a color in Freelance, you use a *color chooser*. A color chooser opens up to display a group of small squares of various colors. All you have to do is select the color you want. You often see color choosers in Freelance Graphics dialog boxes. Regardless of where the color chooser appears, it looks and works the same.

To select a text color from a color chooser (in the text InfoBox, for example), follow these steps:

1. Right-click on a text object and choose Text Block Properties from the shortcut menu. This opens the text InfoBox.

2. Click on the Text color drop-down arrow to open the color chooser. The color chooser contains both SmartMaster colors and color library colors (see Figure 13.1).

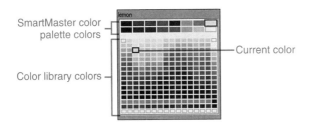

SmartMaster color palette colors

Color library colors

Current color

FIGURE 13.1   You select colors from the color chooser.

3. Click on a color swatch to select a color. The color chooser closes, and the selected color appears in the Text color box and in the object on the page.

4. When you're satisfied with your color choice, click on the Close (X) button to close the InfoBox.

CHANGING THE COLOR PALETTE

The color palette is part of the SmartMaster on which your presentation is based. But you can change the color palette *without* changing the rest of the SmartMaster. To do so, follow these steps:

1. Open the Presentation menu and choose Edit Backdrop to open the SmartMaster for editing.

2. Open the Presentation menu and choose Switch Palette. This opens the Switch Palette dialog box shown in Figure 13.2.

3. Pick a new color palette by clicking on its name in the Palettes list. The Selected palette box changes to show the palette you selected.

4. When you're satisfied with your choice, click OK to close the dialog box. Then click the Done button to close the Current Layout view.

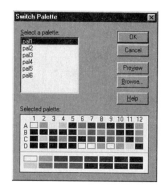

FIGURE 13.2   Use this dialog box to choose a new color palette.

CREATING A COLOR PALETTE

Not only can you change a SmartMaster's color palette by selecting a new palette, but you can edit the palette itself. For instance, if you don't like the SmartMaster's yellow title text, you can substitute white or light gray for that color in the palette. Instantly, all the titles in your presentation change color accordingly.

To edit the color palette, follow these steps:

1. Open the Presentation menu and choose Edit Backdrop to open the SmartMaster for editing.

2. Pull down the Presentation menu again and choose Edit Palette. Freelance opens the Edit Palette dialog box, shown in Figure 13.3.

3. Click on the color in the palette that you want to change.

4. Click on the Change color drop-down arrow to open the color chooser.

5. Pick a new color from the color chooser by clicking on its color swatch. The color chooser closes automatically, and the new color appears in the palette.

6. Repeat steps 3–5 as necessary to further refine your color choice or to edit other colors in the palette.

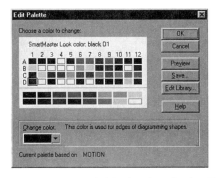

FIGURE 13.3   You change individual colors in the Edit Palette dialog box.

7. (Optional) To save the revised palette so you can use it in other presentations, click on the Save button. In the Save dialog box, enter a name and location to which you want to save it.

8. When you're through, click OK to close the dialog box. Then click the Done button to close Current Layout view.

CREATING A CUSTOM COLOR

As I mentioned earlier, you can redefine any of the 256 colors in Freelance's color library. The standard library even includes 16 spaces for custom colors so you can create a color to match a corporate logo or for other special needs. Once you create a custom color, you can use it as a static color or as part of a SmartMaster color palette.

To create a custom color in the color library, follow these steps:

1. Open the Presentation menu and choose Edit Backdrop to open the SmartMaster for editing.

2. Pull down the Presentation menu again and choose Edit Palette.

3. In the Edit Palette dialog box, click on the Edit Library button. The Edit Library dialog box appears (see Figure 13.4).

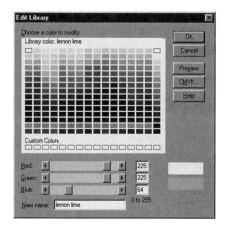

FIGURE 13.4   Create your own custom blended colors.

4. Click on the color swatch you want to change. (The row of color swatches at the bottom of the color library is set aside for custom colors.)

5. Adjust the Red, Green, and Blue sliders to change the color, and watch the change in the color chip to the right.

 What's a Slider?   The *slider* looks and works like a small scroll bar. You can drag the button or click on the arrows at either end to move the button left and right.

6. Type a name for your newly defined color in the New name box.

7. When you finish mixing colors, click OK to close the Edit Library dialog box.

8. Back in the Edit Palette dialog box, you can edit the palette to use your newly defined color if desired. When you finish editing the palette, click OK to close the dialog box.

9. Click Done to close the Current Layout view.

When you save your presentation, Freelance saves the information about color definitions in your presentation file.

VIEWING PAGES IN BLACK & WHITE

Your pages look great displayed on-screen in full color, but how will they print in black and white? Simply printing a gray-scale version of your presentation pages isn't the best answer because the rich colors print as dark, muddy-looking shades of gray. Fortunately, Freelance can automatically make adjustments that will help your pages print better in black and white.

To see what a page will look like when printed in black and white, do one of the following:

- Open the View menu and choose Display in Color. This command is a toggle that switches between a color display and a black-and-white display for your pages.

- Click on the Display in Color button on the status bar. (It's the half color/half gray-scale button just to the left of the Page Layout button.)

In this lesson, you learned how to use Freelance's color selection tools. In the next lesson, you'll learn to create and work with text blocks, which is the first step toward building presentation pages from scratch.

14 ENTERING AND EDITING TEXT

In this lesson, you'll learn how to add text blocks to your page, edit the text in those blocks, and check your spelling.

ADDING A TEXT BLOCK

As you learned in previous lessons, you can create text-based presentation pages by selecting SmartStart content pages or standard layout pages (such as the Bulleted List page layout) and replacing the "Click here" placeholders with your own text. You've also learned that you can create text pages in Outliner view.

But when you need to add text to a presentation page that doesn't fit one of the preformatted page layouts, you need the flexibility and control that's possible only when you add your own text blocks to the page in Current Page view.

To add a text block in Current Page view, follow these steps:

1. Click on the Drawing & Text button to open the drawing tool palette, as shown in Figure 14.1.

2. Click on the Text tool and move the mouse pointer onto the page.

3. Click in the upper-left corner of an imaginary rectangle in which you want to type the text, and drag diagonally downward to create a rectangle that defines the size and position of the text block. When you release the mouse button, a text entry box appears (see Figure 14.2).

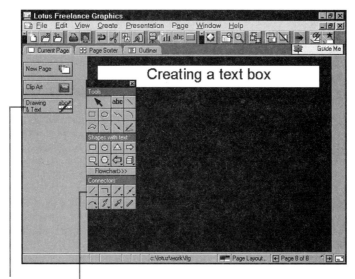

Click this button...   to open this palette.

FIGURE 14.1   The drawing tool palette.

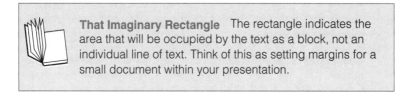

That Imaginary Rectangle   The rectangle indicates the area that will be occupied by the text as a block, not an individual line of text. Think of this as setting margins for a small document within your presentation.

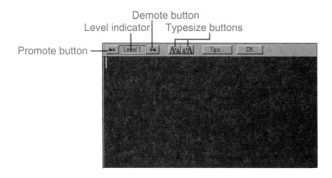

FIGURE 14.2   A sample text entry box.

WORKING IN A TEXT BLOCK

The text entry box should be familiar from Lesson 7 (in which you created a bulleted list). The text entry box for a text block you create with the text tool is no different from those you see when you click on a "Click here" placeholder.

To enter text, just start typing. You can type a word, a single line, a paragraph, or a bulleted list. Use any of the normal text editing features as you're typing your text in the text entry box. You can insert, delete, cut, copy, and paste just as you do in other Windows applications. In addition, you can use any of the following techniques as you enter your presentation text:

Start a New Paragraph or Line   To start a new paragraph or item in a bulleted list, press Enter. If you type a line of text that's too long to fit within the width of the text block, Freelance word wraps the text automatically. You only need to press Enter to start a new paragraph or list item.

Indenting and Levels   Use the Promote and Demote buttons to control the indent level of list items. You can also demote items (indent) by pressing Tab or promote them (unindent) by pressing Shift+Tab.

Selecting Text   To select text for formatting or editing, simply drag the mouse pointer across the text you want to highlight. To select a single word, double-click on it.

Sizing Text   To change the type size of your text, select the text and then click on the Enlarge Typesize or Reduce Typesize button. Each time you click on a button, Freelance makes the selected text one size larger or smaller. If you click on these buttons when no text is selected, Freelance changes the type size of all the text in the text box.

USING THE TEXT RULER

You can display a text ruler to help adjust text indents. It's not part of the default display, though. To activate it, follow these steps:

1. Open the View menu and choose Set View Preferences. The View Preferences dialog box appears.

2. In the Display area, click on the Text block ruler check box.

3. Click OK. The text block ruler appears in the text entry block as shown in Figure 14.3.

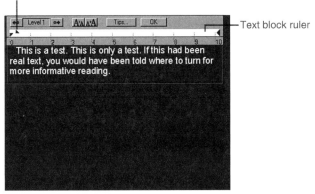

FIGURE 14.3   The text block ruler lets you adjust indents.

Drag the triangular indent markers on the text block ruler to adjust the amount of indent for the selected text level. The top indent marker controls the first line indent in paragraphs with no bullet. For bulleted list items, it controls how far the bullet is indented. The bottom indent marker controls the indent of subsequent lines.

After you enter and edit your text, click on OK. When you close the text entry box, it becomes a text object that's surrounded by selection handles (see Figure 14.4). You can move or manipulate the object.

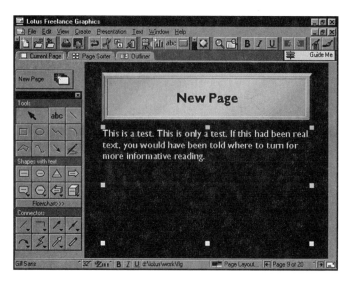

FIGURE 14.4   The selected text object.

MOVING, RESIZING, OR DELETING A TEXT BLOCK

Although the new text block you created may contain several paragraphs or list items, once you close the text entry box, it becomes a single object on your page. Now you manipulate the text block as a unit instead of as individual lines of text. For example, when you move the text block, the entire block moves and all the text inside the block retains its relative position within the block.

> **Making Text Changes**   To change the text within the text block, you must reopen the text entry box and edit the text. To do so, just double-click on the text block.

MOVING A TEXT BLOCK

To move a text block to a new location on the page, follow these steps:

1. If the block is not already selected, click on the text to select the text block.

2. Position the mouse pointer within the confines of the selection handles. Then press the mouse button and drag. The pointer changes to a fist, and a dashed rectangle appears.

3. Drag the rectangle to the new location and release the mouse button to drop the text block there.

CHANGING THE SIZE AND SHAPE OF A TEXT BLOCK

Resizing a text block is like changing the page margins in a word processor document: it doesn't resize the text, it resizes the area defined for the text. The text flows and word-wraps to fit within new boundaries of the text block.

Follow these steps to resize a text block:

1. Select the text block.

2. Click on one of the selection handles surrounding the text block and drag it outward to make the text block larger or inward to make it smaller. A dashed rectangle appears, indicating the boundaries of the resized text block.

3. When you're satisfied with the size, release the mouse button to drop the boundary of the text block in its new position. Freelance redraws the text object at the new size.

DELETING A TEXT BLOCK

Deleting a text block removes the text block and all the text it contains. You do not have to select and delete the text inside the text block separately.

To delete a text block, select it and do one of the following:

- Press the Delete key.

- Open the Edit menu and choose Clear.

CORRECTING SPELLING

A typographical error or misspelled word is bad enough in a memo or letter. It's even more embarrassing when it occurs on a presentation page for all to see. Freelance includes a spelling dictionary to help you find and correct misspelled words in your presentation.

Follow these steps to check the text on your presentation pages for spelling errors:

1. Pull down the Edit menu and choose Check Spelling. Freelance opens the Spell Check dialog box, shown in Figure 14.5.

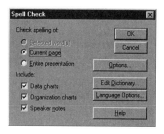

FIGURE 14.5   Start a spell check from this dialog box.

2. Select options to determine the scope of the spell check. You can check a selected word, the current page, or the entire presentation. You can also choose whether you want Freelance to check the text in data charts, organization charts, and speaker notes.

3. Click the OK button to start the spell check.

4. If Freelance finds a word it doesn't recognize, it displays the Spell Check dialog box shown in Figure 14.6.

5. If the word in question is misspelled, do one of these things:

   • Select the correct spelling from the Alternatives list; then click on the Replace button to replace the highlighted word or the Replace All button to replace every occurrence of the word.

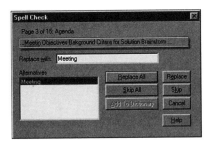

FIGURE 14.6   Fix your spelling errors in this dialog box.

- Type the correct word in the Replace with text box; then click on the Replace button to replace the highlighted word or the Replace All button to replace every occurrence of the word.

If the word in question is spelled correctly but isn't in Freelance's spelling dictionary (which is often true of names and technical terms), do one of these things:

- Click on the Skip button to leave the highlighted word unchanged or the Skip All button to ignore all occurrences of the word during this spell check.

- Click on the Add To Dictionary button to add the word to the auxiliary spelling dictionary so Freelance recognizes the word in future spell checks.

6. Freelance goes on to the next unrecognized word. Repeat step five for each unrecognized word.

7. When Freelance completes the spell check, it displays a small dialog box that says so. Click OK to close the dialog box and end the spell check.

In this lesson, you learned to create text blocks and work with the text you enter in them. You also learned how to find and fix typos and misspellings. In the next lesson, you will learn how to format your text.

15 FORMATTING TEXT

In this lesson, you'll learn how to assign and change the typeface, size, color, and other formatting attributes of your text.

As you will see in this lesson and Lesson 16, Freelance offers several ways to format your text. Which method you use will depend on your own working preferences and on what formatting you need to do at the time.

FORMATTING TEXT WITH THE STATUS BAR BUTTONS

The formatting buttons on the status bar at the bottom of the presentation window give you quick access to common formatting settings. The buttons, shown in Figure 15.1, appear anytime you have text selected—whether you're working in a text entry box or you have a text object selected.

When you use these buttons to format text, the formatting applies to the text you have selected. If a text object is selected, the formatting change applies to all the text in the text block. However, if you open the text entry box and select a specific word or line of text, the formatting is applied to the highlighted text only.

The following list explains the effects of each of the formatting buttons:

> The **Typeface button** displays the current typeface for the selection (or the default typeface if the selection includes more than one typeface). To change the typeface of the selected text or text block, click this button, and select a new typeface from the list of available typefaces (fonts) that appears. The text changes immediately.

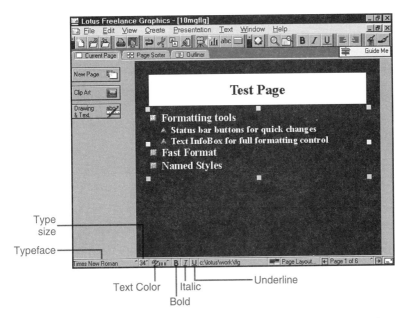

Type
size
Typeface

Text Color   Italic
Bold
Underline

FIGURE 15.1   The formatting buttons appear when you select a text object.

The **Size button** displays the current type size in points. To choose a different size, click on the button, and select a size from the list that appears. If you need a size that's not listed, click on Custom Size. In the resulting dialog box, type a number in the Size in points box and click OK.

The **Text Color button** gives you quick access to a standard color chooser. To change the text color, click on the button, and then click on a color swatch. Freelance changes the color of all the text in the text block. However, it doesn't override any special formatting that you might have applied to a word or line of text within the text block.

The **Bold, Italic, and Underline buttons** toggle on and off the bold, italic, and underline attributes. For example, click on the **Bold** button to make a selected word bold. Click on the button again to toggle the attribute off. You can use a combination of bold, italic, and underline on the same text if you want.

TIP **Alignment**   There's no status bar button for text alignment, but you'll find alignment options on the Text menu.

Changing Text Properties with the InfoBox

For full formatting control, turn to the text InfoBox. The text InfoBox consolidates all formatting options in one dialog box and offers you choices not available anywhere else.

To open the text InfoBox, use either of these methods:

- Select the text, open the Text menu, and choose Text Properties.

- Right-click on the text object or selected text and choose Text Properties from the shortcut menu.

Freelance displays the text InfoBox shown in Figure 15.2. The first thing you need to do in this dialog box is click on the Properties for drop-down list arrow (in the title bar) and select the text level to which you want to apply formatting changes. Then click on the tabs to access the settings you want to change.

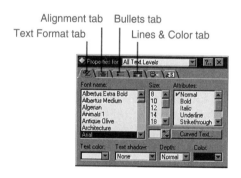

Figure 15.2   The text InfoBox packs a lot of formatting options.

The following section explains how to use the options available in the text InfoBox.

THE INFOBOX OPTIONS

The first tab, the Text Format tab, was shown in Figure 15.2. It duplicates and expands on the formatting options available from the status bar buttons. Table 15.1 tells you how to use the Font and Size options.

TABLE 15.1 THE TEXT FORMAT TAB OPTIONS

OPTION	TO USE IT...
Font name	Pick a typeface from the list of available fonts.
Size	Pick a size from the list or type a custom size into the text box below the Size list.
Attributes	Click on an attribute in the list to turn it on or off (a check mark indicates it's on). Your choices include bold, italic, underline, strikethrough, superscript, and subscript.
Text color	Click on the arrow to open the color chooser and specify the text color.
Text shadow	Select a position from the list for the drop shadow behind the text. Select None for no drop shadow.
Depth	Choose how much separation you want between the text and its shadow.
Color	Click on the arrow to open another color chooser you can use to select the color of the text shadow.

Figure 15.3 shows the Alignment and Spacing tab options. Refer to Table 15.2 to learn how to use the options on this tab.

FIGURE 15.3   Use this tab to set alignment, spacing, and indents.

TABLE 15.2   ALIGNMENT TAB OPTIONS

OPTION	TO USE IT...
Alignment	Click on these buttons to set horizontal and vertical alignment options.
Indent	Type measurements in the 1st Line, Left, and Right Indent boxes if you want to indent the text from the edges of the text block.
Space between	Enter numbers or choose them from these drop-down lists to set the spacing between lines and between paragraphs.

All options pertaining to bullets are on the Bullets tab of the text InfoBox, shown in Figure 15.4. The Bullets tab controls how the bullets in your bulleted lists look.

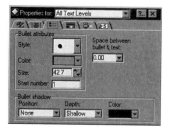

FIGURE 15.4   The Bullets tab.

Table 15.3 gives you the details on how to use these options.

TABLE 15.3 THE BULLETS TAB OPTIONS

OPTION	TO USE IT...
Style	Select the bullet style you want. You can choose from None (for no bullet); letters; numbers; and a variety of dots, boxes, and symbols. Choose Clip Art to open another dialog box, where you can select a clip art symbol to use as the bullet.
Color	Pick a color for the bullets.
Size	Specify the size just as you do for fonts.
Start number	Enter the number or letter for which you want the list to start (in case you want to start numbering from number 12, for example). This box is active only if you choose a number or letter bullet style.
Space between bullet & text	Choose a number of spaces or type a number to tell Freelance how far the text should be from its bullet.
Bullet shadow	Choose settings from these drop-down lists to control the appearance of the bullet's drop shadow. (They work like the text shadow settings.)

Normally, Freelance formats a text block with a transparent background so the text appears against the page background. However, you can give a text block its own background color and a border to create a box around the text. The settings on the Border and Fill tab, shown in Figure 15.5, enable you to control how the box looks.

Figure 15.5   Add a border or fill color to the text block.

Table 15.4 explains how to use the Border and Fill options. Experiment with these options to create just the look you want.

Table 15.4   Lines and Color Tab Options

Option	To Use It...
Style	Pick a border style from the list.
Width	Pick a border width from the list.
Color	Select a border color from the color chooser.
Shadow	Choose a drop shadow position from the list. (There are no shadow color or depth settings.)
Background	Specify a fill color to appear behind the text.
Pattern	Select a fill pattern from the list. Select the default, None, to allow the page background to show through. (Hatch patterns and graduated shading effects are also available.)
Pattern color	Choose the second color you want Freelance to use in shading or hatching effects (if you choose anything other than None or a solid color in the Pattern box).

Any changes you make in the text InfoBox take effect immediately. When you finish making formatting adjustments, click on the InfoBox's Close (X) button to close the dialog box.

CHANGING THE TYPEFACE GLOBALLY

Suppose you finish your presentation only to hear, "The presentation looks great, but you should use the corporate typeface when you present it to the board." This sort of suggestion is all too common. Although it could mean hours of work reformatting every page, Freelance's capability to change the typeface (font) for the entire presentation with a single command makes it easy.

To change the typeface throughout your presentation, follow these steps:

1. Open the Presentation menu and choose Change the Typeface Globally. Freelance opens the Change Typeface Globally dialog box.

2. In the list box at the top, pick a new typeface from the list of fonts available on your system. The font you choose is used in the text blocks on all pages of your presentation.

3. (Optional) If you want to use a different typeface in charts, tables, and organization charts, check those options in the lower part of the dialog box.

4. Click OK. A dialog box appears, warning you that the change will affect all the pages in the presentation. It also affects named styles (which you'll learn about in the next lesson). You cannot undo a global typeface change.

5. Click OK to confirm the change. Freelance changes the typeface for all text (except that to which you have previously applied manual typeface changes).

In this lesson, you learned how to control the details of text formatting on your presentation pages. In the next lesson, you'll learn how to use Fast Formats and named styles to simplify formatting.

16 USING FAST FORMAT AND NAMED STYLES

In this lesson, you'll learn how to copy formatting from one text object to another, and how to use named styles to format text.

COPYING FORMATTING WITH FAST FORMAT

In Lesson 15, you learned how to use Freelance's formatting tools to control the appearance of a text object. But you don't have to repeat the somewhat laborious process of adjusting the formatting for each text object you create.

Once you get one text object formatted the way you like it, you can use Freelance's Fast Format feature to copy that object's text properties (typeface, size, alignment, bullets, and so forth) and apply them to other text objects. It's a lot like using the Copy and Paste commands and the Windows Clipboard, except that you copy formatting attributes instead of actual text.

To copy the text properties from one object and apply them to another object, follow these steps:

1. Select the text object that's already formatted to your liking (whose text properties you want to copy).

2. Open the Text menu, choose Fast Format, and then choose Pick Up Attributes. Freelance copies the formatting information from the selected text and stores it in temporary memory.

3. Select the text object you want to format (the one you want to apply text properties *to).*

4. Open the Text menu, choose Fast Format, and then choose Apply Attributes. Freelance reformats the selected text with the text properties copied from the first text object.

5. Repeat steps 3 and 4 to apply the same formatting to any other text objects you want.

Fast Format May Reformat More Than You Expect
You can't use Fast Format to apply formatting to just the selected text within a text entry box. Fast Format applies the formatting attributes to all the text in the entire text block.

WHAT IS A NAMED STYLE?

If you use a particular set of text properties frequently, you can create a *named style*. Freelance lets you define a set of text properties and save them with a name so you can format any text object with those text properties simply by applying the named style. And if at any time you redefine the text properties assigned to a named style, Freelance automatically reformats all text objects using that style with its new properties.

Although you don't know it, you already have some named styles. SmartMasters use named styles to format the text in "Click here" placeholders. Each SmartMaster includes six named styles:

- Presentation title
- Presentation subtitle
- Page title
- Bulleted text
- Numbered list
- Label text

When you choose a new SmartMaster for a presentation, Freelance changes the text formatting throughout the presentation by changing the text properties associated with each of these standard named styles.

You can create and apply your own named styles or any of the six standard named styles to the text objects on your presentation pages. You can use named styles with text in "Click here" placeholders, diagrams, shapes, and the text objects you create with the text tool. However, you can't use named styles to format text in charts and tables.

Applying a Style to an Object

To apply a named style to a text object, follow these steps:

1. Select the text object to which you want to apply the style.

2. Open the Text menu, choose Named Styles, and then choose Apply. The text InfoBox appears, with the Styles tab in front (see Figure 16.1).

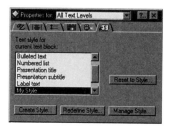

Figure 16.1 Named styles, like other formatting options, are found in the text InfoBox.

3. Click on the name of the style you want to apply. Freelance immediately applies it to the selected text block.

4. Click on the Close (X) button to close the text InfoBox.

CREATING AND REDEFINING STYLES

To create a named style, follow these steps:

1. Select any text block.

2. Open the Text menu and choose Text Properties to open the text InfoBox.

3. Change the formatting settings as necessary to give the text block the properties you want to define as a style.

4. Click on the Styles tab.

5. Click on the Create Style button, and Freelance displays the Create Text Style dialog box shown in Figure 16.2.

FIGURE 16.2   This dialog box shows a sample of the formatting style you've created.

6. In the text box, type a unique name for the style. The name can contain up to 32 characters (letters, numbers, and spaces).

7. Click OK to close the Create Text Style dialog box and add the style to the list in the text InfoBox.

8. Click on the Close (X) button to close the text InfoBox.

To redefine the text properties assigned to an existing named style, follow these steps:

1. Select a text block that uses the style you want to redefine.

2. Open the Text menu and choose Text Properties to open the text InfoBox.

3. Change the formatting settings on the text InfoBox tabs as necessary. (Lesson 15 describes these formatting options in detail.)

4. When the selected text block looks the way you want it to, you need to save the changes. Click on the Styles tab.

5. Click on the Redefine Style button, and Freelance displays the Redefine Style dialog box.

6. Click OK to close the dialog box and return to the text InfoBox. Freelance updates the text properties of every text block in your presentation that uses the named style you redefined.

7. Click on the Close (X) button to close the text InfoBox.

 TIP   **Breaking the Ties to a Named Style**   You can prevent future changes to a style's definition from affecting the text properties of a text block. After you apply the named style to the text block, repeat the steps for applying the style but choose the style None. This doesn't change the text properties that are already applied, but it breaks the link between the text block and the named style.

Managing Named Styles

When you save your presentation, the named styles you've created for that presentation are saved in the file along with the pages and other information. However, that does not limit you to using the named styles in that presentation only.

You can bring a named style that you created in one presentation into your current presentation and use it to format text blocks. Although you can't copy styles from one presentation to another directly, you can copy a text object (see Lesson 12) or a page (see Lesson 10) containing a style. When you do, Freelance adds the style to the list of styles available in the current presentation.

There may also come a time when you decide you don't have any more need for a named style you've created. If you need to delete a style from a presentation, follow these steps:

1. Select any text object.

2. Open the Text menu, choose Named Styles, and then choose Manage. The Manage Styles dialog box appears.

3. Select the style you want to delete and click on the Delete button. If the style is used by text objects in your presentation, Freelance displays a warning dialog box. Click OK to confirm the deletion.

OVERRIDING STYLES

Applying a style to a text object sets the text properties for that object. However, you can override the style by manually applying formatting attributes to portions of a text object. The style itself remains unaffected; it still applies to the rest of the text in the text block and to all other text blocks using the style.

 TIP **Removing Style Overrides**   If you want to remove formatting overrides in a text block, select the text object, open the text InfoBox, click on the Style tab, and click on the Reset to Style button.

In this lesson, you learned to pick up and apply formatting and to use named styles. In the next lesson, you'll learn how to create charts such as bar charts, line charts, and pie charts.

CREATING CHARTS

In this lesson, you'll learn to create data-driven charts to make your numbers easier to understand.

Charts can be invaluable aids for making numerical data easier to understand. By providing graphical representations of numerical information, charts enable your audience to see relationships and trends without having to exert the effort to study and interpret the raw data.

CHART TYPES

Freelance allows you to create several chart types to serve a wide range of needs. In addition, you can choose variations such as horizontal or vertical orientation and 3D treatments for most of the chart types. Freelance offers the following basic chart types:

Bar	Pie
Stacked Bar	Hi/Low/Close/Open
100% Stacked Bar	XY (Scatter)
Line	Radar
Area	Mixed
Number Grid	

Despite the range of chart types Freelance offers, the process for creating them is basically the same. You follow the same steps to create a bar chart, a pie chart, or any other type of chart. Of course, you need to enter slightly different information for the various chart types, but Freelance changes the dialog boxes to reflect those differences. For example, if you select the Pie chart type, you won't see options in the Edit Titles dialog box for entering X and Y axis labels because a pie chart does not have X and Y axes.

The examples in this lesson walk you through creating a simple bar chart. If you create a different type of chart, some of the dialog boxes will look slightly different.

CREATING A CHART

In many ways, a chart is similar to the kind of text block you use for a bulleted list. It's a large block that you can size and position on your presentation page as a single unit. You use dialog boxes to edit and format the contents of the chart object.

To create a chart, you follow these basic steps (the details of which you'll learn in the rest of the lesson):

1. Add a chart object to your presentation page.

2. Select the chart type you want to create.

3. Enter (or import) the chart data.

4. Add title and label text.

Freelance generates the chart from the data you supply. You can move, resize, and edit the finished chart as necessary.

ADDING A CHART TO YOUR PAGE

To add a chart object to a presentation page, do one of the following:

- Create a new presentation page using one of the standard layouts that includes a chart. Then click on the Click here to... placeholder to begin defining the chart.

- From an existing presentation page, pull down the Create menu and choose Chart.

Freelance opens the Create Chart dialog box, shown in Figure 17.1.

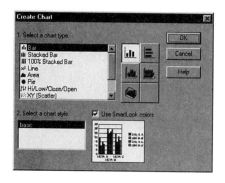

FIGURE 17.1   The Create Chart dialog box.

SELECTING THE CHART TYPE

The first decision you must make is what kind of chart you want to create. You select a chart type from the Create Chart dialog box. To do so, follow these steps:

1. Click on the chart type you want in the number 1 list box. The buttons to the right of the list box change to display the variations for that particular chart type.

2. Click on a button to select a variation of the chart type (such as horizontal orientation or 3D bars).

3. Click OK to close the Create Chart dialog box.

 I Chose the Wrong One!   Don't worry if you select the wrong chart type to begin with. You can switch to another chart type later, and Freelance will preserve all your data and adjust it to apply to the new chart type.

ENTERING DATA

When you select the chart type, Freelance opens the Edit Data dialog box (see Figure 17.2).

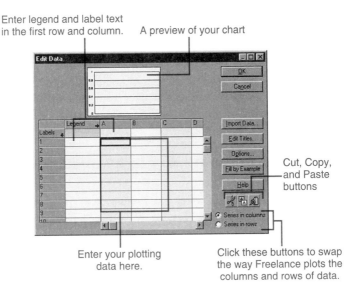

Enter legend and label text in the first row and column.   A preview of your chart

Cut, Copy, and Paste buttons

Enter your plotting data here.

Click these buttons to swap the way Freelance plots the columns and rows of data.

FIGURE 17.2   The Edit Data dialog box.

You enter the data for your chart in the table section of this dialog box. As you enter your data, the sample chart at the top of the dialog box gives you a preview of the chart you are creating.

There are two ways to enter data for a chart. You can enter the data into the dialog box, or you can import data from a spreadsheet file.

TYPING DATA

The most straightforward way to enter chart data is to type it directly into the cells of the data table. (A *cell* is the intersection of a row and a column in a table or spreadsheet.) You simply click on a cell and type. To move to another cell, use the arrow keys or click on the cell you want to go to.

TIP

Save Typing You can copy data from another presentation page or another program and paste it into the Edit
Data dialog box using the Cut, Copy, and Paste toolbar
buttons or the keyboard shortcuts for those commands
(Ctrl+X, Ctrl+C, and Ctrl+V, respectively).

IMPORTING DATA FROM A SPREADSHEET

There's a good chance that the data you want to use for a chart
already exists in a spreadsheet file. Freelance allows you to use
that data without reentering it. To import data from a spreadsheet
file into a Freelance chart, follow these steps:

1. In the Edit Data dialog box, click on the Import Data
   button. The Open dialog box appears.

2. To select the spreadsheet file from which you want to
   import data, navigate through folders and adjust the file
   type as necessary. When you find the file, click on it and
   click Open. Freelance opens the Edit Links dialog box and
   displays the selected file (see Figure 17.3).

3. Scroll through the viewing window to display the portion
   of the spreadsheet file you want to import. Click and drag
   to highlight the range of spreadsheet cells that you want
   to import as plotting data.

4. Click on the Data button. Freelance inserts the range
   description in the Data field.

5. Repeat steps 3 and 4 to import spreadsheet cells for the
   chart Title, Legend, and X Axis Labels. (You can leave one
   or more of the ranges blank and define those values later.)

6. When you finish identifying ranges to import, click OK.
   Freelance returns to the Edit Data dialog box.

A preview of the chart

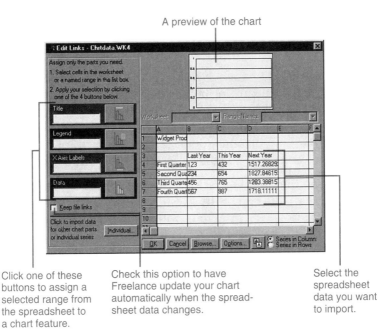

Click one of these
buttons to assign a
selected range from
the spreadsheet to
a chart feature.

Check this option to have
Freelance update your chart
automatically when the spreadsheet data changes.

Select the
spreadsheet
data you want
to import.

FIGURE 17.3   The Edit Links dialog box.

ADDING TITLES

Although the heart of a chart is the plotting data, most charts also
need some text labels to put the numbers into context. You can
create labels (Freelance calls them titles) for the chart, the X axis,
and the Y axis. To add titles to your chart, click on the Edit Titles
button in the Edit Data dialog box. Freelance opens the Edit Titles
dialog box.

This dialog box provides space for a three-line chart title, a three-
line note that will appear beneath the chart, and one-line titles
for the X axis, Y axis, and 2Y axis (if there is one in your chart).
To add a title, simply click on a text box and type in the text.
The sample chart gives you a preview of the effect you're creating.
When you're satisfied with the titles, click on the Edit Data button to return to the Edit Data dialog box.

WORKING WITH THE COMPLETED CHART

When you finish defining the chart, click OK in either the Edit Data or the Edit Titles dialog box. Freelance closes the dialog box and generates the chart. The chart automatically appears on your presentation page. The chart may not automatically be sized and positioned on your presentation page the way you want it. Fortunately, you can resize and move it just like any other object.

First click on the chart to select it (if it's not already selected). To resize the chart, drag one of its selection handles. Freelance redraws the chart and its titles to fit within the newly defined area. To move the chart, simply click and drag it to its new location.

Remember This! When selecting or moving a chart as a whole, be sure to click on the background of the chart and not on one of the chart elements.

If, after seeing the full-size chart, you decide that you need to revise some of the settings, you can do so easily.

- To revise chart data, right-click on the chart and choose Edit Data from the shortcut menu. Freelance reopens the Edit Data dialog box. Change the settings as necessary and click OK. Freelance closes the dialog box and revises the chart.

- To change the chart type, right-click on the chart and choose Chart Type from the shortcut menu. Freelance opens the Properties for Chart InfoBox. Select a different chart type or variation, and then click on the Close (X) button to close the InfoBox.

In this lesson, you learned how to create charts. In the next lesson, you'll learn how to edit and customize those charts.

WORKING WITH CHART ELEMENTS

In this lesson, you'll learn how to customize the standard Freelance-generated charts to get the effects you want.

CUSTOMIZING CHARTS

Freelance does a decent job of creating an attractive chart based on your data and its default settings. However, in some cases, you may want to use different fonts and colors, change the scaling of an axis, or adjust the position of a title or legend. To accommodate those needs, Freelance allows you to control formatting and other details for most of the chart elements.

You can adjust nearly all aspects of a chart's appearance with the settings in Freelance's InfoBox. To work with the InfoBox, follow these steps:

1. Right-click anywhere on the chart.

2. Choose the top item (Chart Properties, Title Properties, etc.) from the shortcut menu. Freelance opens the InfoBox (see Figure 18.1) showing the properties for the chart element you right-clicked on.

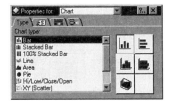

FIGURE 18.1 The InfoBox options control nearly all aspects of a chart's appearance.

3. Click on the chart element you want to change, and the InfoBox displays the options available for that element. The InfoBox may contain several tabs of options you can use to control different aspects of the selected element.

4. Select a tab and adjust the appropriate settings. The chart changes immediately to reflect the changes you make. Adjust the settings on the other InfoBox tabs as necessary.

Undo   If you don't like the effect of a change you make in the InfoBox, you don't have to remember the old setting to change it back. Just pull down the Edit menu and choose Undo Setting Change to revert to the previous setting.

5. Repeat steps 3 and 4 to format any other chart elements.

6. When you finish formatting your chart, click on the Close (X) button.

The InfoBox contains hundreds of options and settings for charts. We can't list them all in this book, but the following examples will demonstrate how to perform some of the more common chart formatting tasks.

Adding a Border Around the Chart

The entire chart sits on a rectangular background. By default, the chart background is transparent, which makes it invisible on your presentation page. However, you can give the chart a background color and border to make it stand out from the rest of the page by following these steps:

1. Open the InfoBox. Then click on the Properties for drop-down arrow (in the InfoBox's title bar) and choose Chart (or simply double-click on the chart background).

2. Click on the Lines & Colors tab (the third tab from the left) to display the options shown in Figure 18.2.

FIGURE 18.2   These settings control the appearance of the background.

3. In the Border area, open the Style drop-down list and choose a border style (probably the solid line). Then select appropriate settings in the Width and Color drop-down lists.

4. In the Interior area, uncheck the Same color as border option. Open the Pattern drop-down list and choose a setting, such as the solid box. Select colors in the Pattern color and Background drop-down lists.

5. Select values for the Shadow and Rounding options if you want a drop shadow behind the chart or rounded corners on the chart background.

6. Select another chart element to modify, or click the Close (X) button to close the InfoBox.

CONTROLLING AXES

Freelance automatically sets a chart's Y-axis scale to accommodate the values you're plotting. But you may prefer to use a different scale. For instance, you could follow these steps to adjust the Y-axis scale of the current chart to match another chart so you can compare the two charts.

1. Open the InfoBox. Then click on the Properties for drop-down list arrow and choose Y-axis, or click on the Y-axis of the chart (the numbers labeling the axis values or one of the grid lines).

2. Click on the Scale tab to display the options shown in Figure 18.3.

FIGURE 18.3   Adjust the Y-axis scale using these settings.

3. To override Freelance's automatic axis scaling, click on the Maximum check box. Then click on the text box to the right of the word Maximum, and type in a new number. Press Enter or click on another option, and Freelance redraws the chart using the new scale value.

4. Adjust the other settings on the Scale tab to fine-tune the axis scaling as necessary.

5. You can use other tabs in this InfoBox to control such details as the frequency and color of tick marks and grid lines.

TIP   **Edit the Title from Here**   The Titles tab includes a text box where you can edit the Y-axis title without returning to the Edit Titles dialog box.

6. Select any other chart element you want to change, or click the Close (X) button to close the InfoBox.

USING CHART STYLES

After modifying a chart to get it just the way you want it, you can save those settings in a chart style. When you create a chart style, Freelance saves chart formatting information (such as chart colors, and the size and font you chose for title text) in a special file on your hard disk. Then when you want to use the same settings for another chart, you can simply apply the chart style to the new chart instead of adjusting all the settings manually.

To create a chart style, follow these steps:

1. Select the chart that you want to use as the template for the chart style. Make sure all the settings are adjusted the way you want them.

2. Pull down the Chart menu, click on Chart Style, and choose Create from the flyout menu. Freelance opens the Create Chart Style dialog box.

3. Click OK, and Freelance opens the Save As dialog box.

4. Type a name for the chart style in the File name box.

5. Click on the Save button to record the chart settings in the chart style file.

Once you've created a chart style, follow these steps to apply those same settings to a new chart:

1. Select the chart to which you want to apply the chart style.

2. Pull down the Chart menu, click on Chart Style, and choose Apply from the flyout menu. Freelance opens the Properties for Chart InfoBox to the Style tab, shown in Figure 18.4.

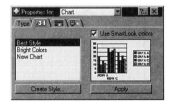

FIGURE 18.4   Apply a chart style to apply many settings at once.

3. Select a chart style from the list. The sample on the right gives you a preview of those settings on a generic chart.

4. Select the Use SmartLook colors check box if you want to use the presentation's SmartMaster color palette. (Deselect the check box if you want to use the colors saved in the chart style.)

Look Elsewhere! If the chart style you want doesn't appear in the list (or no chart styles appear at all), you may need to tell Freelance to look in another folder on your hard drive for the chart style files. Pull down the Chart menu, click Chart Style, and choose Change Path. Use the Open dialog box that appears to locate the correct folder and file.

5. Click the Apply button to apply the settings from the chart style to the selected chart.

6. Click the Close (X) button to close the InfoBox.

FROM HERE...

As I said earlier in the lesson, the previous sections outline only a few of the chart formatting changes you can make using the InfoBox options. Here are a few others you can try.

- If you don't like the position or color of the Legend box, you can change it using the options on the Options tab of the Properties for Legend InfoBox.

- You can change the color of a bar or a pie slice in a chart by using the options on the Line & Fill tab of the Properties for Series InfoBox. You might want to make the second series of bars in a chart red to tie in with a product logo, for example.

- You can choose whether to hide or display any individual chart element. For example, if you want to hide the X-axis title "Months" that appears below a string of month names (which *is* redundant), you can do so by removing the check mark from the Show title check box on the Titles tab of the Properties for X-axis InfoBox.

Don't let this lesson limit your modifications. Experiment with the other InfoBox options, and refer to Freelance's documentation or online Help system for more details.

In this lesson, you learned how to customize your Freelance-created data-driven charts by manipulating the elements that make up the charts. In the next lesson, you'll learn how to create another common type of chart: an organization chart.

LESSON 19

CREATING AND EDITING ORGANIZATION CHARTS

In this lesson, you'll learn how to create and edit organization charts.

CREATING AN ORGANIZATION CHART

Organization charts are diagrams that show the reporting hierarchy of a company, organization, department, or team. They are common elements in presentations because they help people visualize the relationships between the persons or organizations involved in a project. Freelance includes a feature that creates organization charts automatically from the data you enter.

To create an organization chart, follow these steps:

1. Open the Create menu and choose Organization Chart to add an organization chart to an existing page. Freelance displays the Organization Chart Gallery dialog box, shown in Figure 19.1.

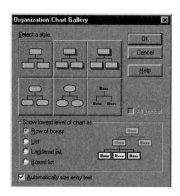

FIGURE 19.1   The Organization Chart Gallery dialog box.

Use a Standard Page Layout   If you created a new page using the Organization Chart page layout, you can simply click on the Click here placeholder to get to the Organization Chart Gallery dialog box and begin creating the chart.

2. Select a layout for your organization chart by clicking on one of the style buttons. At the bottom of the dialog box, indicate how you want the bottom level of the chart treated. Then click OK to proceed to the Organization Chart Entry List dialog box (see Figure 19.2).

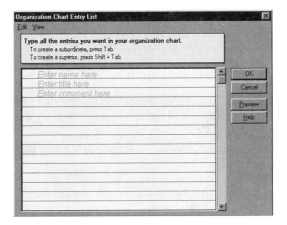

FIGURE 19.2   The Organization Chart Entry List dialog box.

3. First you enter the information that goes in the box at the very top of your organization chart. Type the name, title, and comment, pressing Enter after each one. When you press Enter after typing the comment, Freelance automatically creates placeholders for the first subordinate entry's information, which is indented from the top entry's information.

4. Continue to add entries to the data list for the organization chart.

5. The data list is organized as an outline with subordinates indented under the higher-level entry to which they report. To indent an entry, place the cursor anywhere within the entry text and press Tab. To promote an entry to a higher level, press Shift+Tab.

Kill the Comments The organization chart contains three placeholders for each entry: Name, Title, and Comment. You don't have to display all three. You can open the View menu and choose Names Only, Names and Titles, or All to set which of these you want displayed.

6. When you finish entering data, click OK to close the dialog box. Freelance generates the organization chart and displays it on your page. Figure 19.3 shows a sample organization chart.

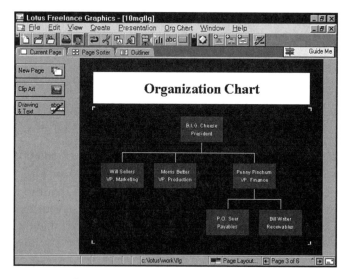

FIGURE 19.3 An organization chart generated by Freelance.

EDITING AND REFINING AN ORGANIZATION CHART

It's a rare accomplishment to create an organization chart that looks the way you want it to on the first try. More often than not, you'll need to edit the entries and make other changes to the layout and appearance.

CHANGING THE LAYOUT

To change the organization chart's layout, follow these steps:

1. Right-click on the chart and choose Organization Chart Properties from the shortcut menu that appears.

2. Click on the Layout tab of the InfoBox to display the options shown in Figure 19.4. (If the Layout tab isn't available at first, click on the Properties for drop-down arrow and choose Organization Chart.)

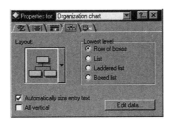

FIGURE 19.4   Choose a new layout for your organization chart.

3. Click on the arrow button beside the sample layout to display the layout choices. Then click on the layout you want to use. The chart reflects the change immediately.

4. Adjust other settings as necessary, and then click on the Close (X) button to close the InfoBox.

CHANGING THE TEXT

Freelance gives you two ways to change the text entries in your organization chart. You can return to the Organization Chart Entry List dialog box and add to or edit the chart data, or you can edit existing entries directly on the chart.

To reopen the Organization Chart Entry List dialog box, do one of the following:

- Right-click on the chart and choose Edit Data from the shortcut menu that appears.

- Select the chart, open the Org Chart menu, and choose Edit Data.

- From the Layout tab of the Properties for Organization chart InfoBox, click on the Edit data button.

Rearranging Entries   To rearrange the order of the entries in the Organization Chart Entry List dialog box, click on the bullet for an entry to highlight it, and then drag the bullet up or down the list to a new location.

To edit text entries directly on the chart, follow these steps:

1. Select the chart.

2. Click on the entry you want to change. A text insertion point cursor appears, and a rectangle surrounds the text.

3. Edit the text.

4. When you finish editing, click anywhere on the page to deselect the text.

Breaking Long Lines   If you need to break a long title or any other line of text so that it fits on two lines, select the entry and position the cursor at the point where you want to break the line. Then press Ctrl+Enter.

CHANGING THE APPEARANCE OF THE ORGANIZATION CHART

You can exercise a great deal of control over the appearance of your organization charts. You can change colors, typefaces, the thickness of connecting lines, and so on. You make all these changes by using the Properties for Organization chart InfoBox.

To change the appearance of the organization chart, follow these steps:

1. Right-click on the part of the chart you want to change and choose Organization Chart Properties from the short-cut menu that appears. Freelance opens the Properties for Organization chart InfoBox.

2. Click the Properties for drop-down arrow and choose the portion of the chart to which you want to apply the changes. For instance, you can choose to make changes in the entire chart, just the current box, or the current box and its peers.

3. Change the settings on the various tabs as necessary. Freelance makes the changes in the chart immediately.

4. When you finish modifying the chart, click on the Close (X) button to close the Properties for Organization chart InfoBox.

In this lesson, you learned how to add organization charts to your presentation pages and modify them to meet your needs. In the next lesson, you'll learn how to create other kinds of diagrams and flow charts.

20 ADDING DIAGRAMS

In this lesson, you'll learn how to add Freelance's ready-made diagrams to your presentation pages and how to create your own custom diagrams.

USING READY-MADE DIAGRAMS

Freelance comes with a library of ready-made diagrams suitable for a variety of uses. Adding one of the ready-made diagrams to your presentation page is quick and easy. Simply follow these steps:

1. Switch to Current Page view and go to the page to which you want to add the diagram.

2. Open the Create menu and choose Drawing/Diagram. The Add Diagram dialog box appears.

 TIP **Click Here to Create Diagram** If you create a new page using the Diagram layout, you can click on the "Click here" placeholder to open the Add Diagram dialog box. From there, the process of creating a diagram is the same as if you chose Drawing/Diagram from the Create menu.

3. Click on Use a ready-made diagram, and then click OK. Freelance displays the Add Clip Art or Diagram to the Page dialog box (also known as the Diagram Library), shown in Figure 20.1.

4. Pick a category from the drop-down list.

Select a category here.

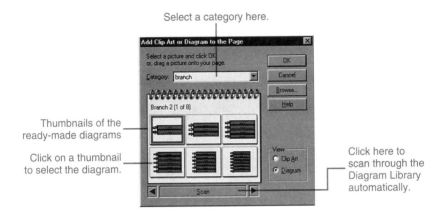

Thumbnails of the
ready-made diagrams

Click on a thumbnail
to select the diagram.

Click here to
scan through the
Diagram Library
automatically.

FIGURE 20.1 The Diagram Library.

5. Use the left and right arrows next to the Scan button to scroll through the diagrams in the selected category.

6. Click on the thumbnail of the diagram you want to add to your page.

7. Click OK to close the dialog box. Freelance adds the diagram to your page. On your presentation page, the diagram is selected (see Figure 20.2) so you can move, resize, or edit it as you would any other object or group of objects.

After you add a diagram to your page, you need to insert text in the various boxes to label the diagram elements. For convenience, the ready-made diagrams include placeholder text similar to the "Click here" placeholders you've seen elsewhere. To replace that text with your own, follow these steps:

1. Click on the diagram to select it (if it's not already selected).

2. Click on the placeholder text you want to replace. A box opens, containing a flashing text insertion point.

3. Type the text.

4. To close the text entry box, click on another text placeholder or anywhere outside the diagram.

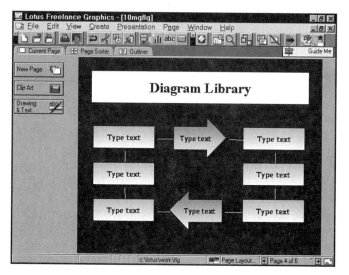

FIGURE 20.2 The ready-made diagram on your presentation page.

CREATING CUSTOM DIAGRAMS

If you can't find a ready-made diagram in the diagram library to fit your needs, you can create your own custom diagram. Freelance provides the basic building blocks of diagrams: a wide assortment of shapes and connectors that you can arrange on your page to build a diagram. And to make creating a diagram even easier, Freelance includes a palette of "Shapes with text"— shapes that contain built-in text blocks to label the diagram blocks. When you move or resize a shape, the text block goes with it automatically.

The following steps give you an overview of creating a custom diagram. You don't know how to perform some of these tasks yet, but they are explained in detail in the following sections.

1. Open the page to which you want to add a custom diagram and switch to Current Page view if necessary.

2. Click on the Drawing & Text button to open the Drawing & Text tool palette (see Figure 20.3).

FIGURE 20.3 This palette contains shapes and connectors for building a custom diagram.

3. Add shapes with text to the page. (You can size and arrange the shapes to meet your own needs, as you'll learn in the next few sections.)

4. Edit the text in the shapes just as you would if you were working with a ready-made diagram.

5. Add shapes and connectors between shapes, and edit text as needed to complete the diagram.

ADDING SHAPES WITH TEXT

To add a shape with text to your page, follow these steps:

1. Click on a shape tool in the Drawing & Text tool palette. Clicking on some shape tools opens a sub-palette of additional choices; pick the specific shape you want to draw.

2. Position the pointer on the page and click and drag to define the approximate size and position of the shape. The selected shape appears, with a text block inside.

3. Move and resize the shape as necessary.

4. Click in the middle of the selected shape to open a text entry box for the linked text.

5. Type the text to go inside the shape and click OK.

CHANGING ATTRIBUTES OF SHAPES WITH TEXT

If you don't like the default color of the shape or the text formatting, you can change either of those attributes as well as many others. To do so, follow these steps:

1. Right-click on the shape you want to change and choose Text Shape Properties from the shortcut menu that appears.

2. In the Properties for Text Shape InfoBox, adjust the formatting settings as necessary. The changes take effect immediately.

3. Click on the Close (X) button to close the InfoBox.

TIP   **Fitting Text Inside Shapes**   You can instruct Freelance to automatically adjust the type size so that the text fits within the shape. Simply open the Properties for Text Shape InfoBox, click on the Basics tab, and check the Shrink shape text to fit shape check box.

CHANGING THE SHAPE TYPE

To convert a shape with text from one shape type to another, follow these steps:

1. Right-click on the shape to open the shortcut menu.

2. Choose Switch Text Shape Type, and a flyout menu appears. Click on the button for the new shape type.

ADDING CONNECTORS

Adding connecting lines, arrows, and pipes between shapes is easy. Just follow these steps:

1. Pick a general connector type by clicking on a connector tool in the Drawing & Text tool palette.

2. Pick a specific connector type from the additional choices Freelance offers.

3. Click on the first shape you want to connect and drag to the second shape. (You don't have to click precisely on the edges of the shapes; Freelance aligns the connector with the edges of the shapes.)

4. When the pointer is on the second shape, release the mouse button. Freelance draws the connector between the two shapes.

5. Repeat these steps as needed to connect other shapes.

In this lesson, you learned how to use ready-made diagrams and how to use Freelance's tools to create custom diagrams. In the next lesson, you'll learn how to add tables to your presentation pages.

21

CREATING TABLES

In this lesson, you'll learn how to create and format tables.

A *table* is a collection of numbers or text organized into columns and rows of information. It seems that every presentation includes at least one or two tables. Freelance includes a solid set of tools for creating and manipulating tables.

ADDING A TABLE TO A PAGE

To create a presentation page containing a table, do one of the following:

- Create a new page using the Table page layout, and then click on the Click here to create table box.

- Starting with an existing presentation page, pull down the Create menu, and choose Table.

Freelance opens the Table Gallery dialog box shown in Figure 21.1.

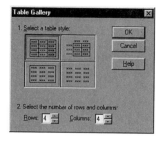

FIGURE 21.1   The Table Gallery dialog box.

Click on one of the four table style buttons to choose which cells (if any) will have borders. Then specify the number of rows and columns you want in the table either by typing numbers in the Rows and Columns boxes or by adjusting the numbers with the up and down arrow buttons beside each box. Click OK, and Freelance creates an empty table according to your specifications.

If you don't like the position of the table on the page, you can click on it and drag it to where you want it. You can also adjust the size of the table by dragging on one of the small square handles that surround the table when it's selected. Drag a handle toward the center of the table to make the table smaller; drag the handle away from the center to enlarge the table.

ADDING DATA TO A TABLE

Your next task is to add data to the table. You can add text or numeric data to any cell of the table. To add data to the table, follow these steps:

1. Click once on the table to select it (if it isn't already selected).

2. Click on the table again to begin editing it. During editing, Freelance surrounds the table with a thick gray border, and a flashing insertion point appears in one of the table cells.

3. To begin entering data, click on the cell where you want to enter text or numbers, and begin typing. You can press Enter to add another line of data in a cell. Freelance enlarges the cell automatically to accommodate any additional lines.

4. To move to the next cell, press Tab or one of the arrow keys.

5. Continue entering data until you complete the table. Figure 21.2 shows the table during editing.

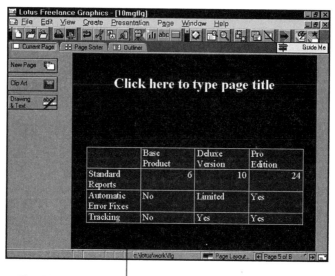

The thick border appears when you're editing.

Figure 21.2   Editing the table data.

Save Typing   You can copy data from another program and paste it into your table. To do so, open the source document in the other program, select the data to copy, open the Edit menu and choose Copy. Then switch to Freelance, select the table, and click on it again to begin editing. Drag across the cells of the table to highlight the area to which you want to add data. Finally, open the Edit menu and choose Paste. Freelance inserts data from the Windows Clipboard in the highlighted cells of the table.

Don't Forget!   When you copy and paste data from another application to a Freelance table, you must highlight the block of cells where you want the data to appear before you use the Paste command. If you don't, all the pasted data goes into one cell.

WORKING WITH COLUMNS AND ROWS

Consider this common scenario: You think you have all the data for a table entered...but then the boss calls with a list of changes. No problem. Freelance lets you add, delete, and move columns and rows to rearrange the information in a table.

ADDING COLUMNS AND ROWS TO A TABLE

To add a single row of new cells to the chart, follow these steps:

1. Select a cell in the row above where you want to add the new row.

2. Open the Table menu, click on Insert, and choose Row from the flyout menu.

3. Freelance inserts a row of empty cells below the selected cell.

 TIP **Inserting Columns** Inserting a column is just like inserting a row except you choose Column from the flyout menu instead of Row.

Follow these steps to insert multiple rows or columns:

1. Select a cell adjacent to where you want to insert the new rows or columns.

2. Pull down the Table menu, click on Insert, and choose Row/Column. Freelance opens the Insert Column/Row dialog box, shown in Figure 21.3.

3. Click on Column or Row, and specify the number of columns or rows you want to insert.

4. Click on Before or After to indicate where the new rows or columns should be inserted in relation to the current cell.

5. Click OK, and Freelance inserts the rows or columns you requested.

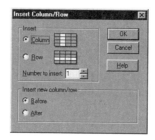

FIGURE 21.3 The Insert Column/Row dialog box.

DELETING COLUMNS AND ROWS

When you need to delete a row or column of cells from a table, follow these steps:

1. With the chart selected, click in any cell in the row or column you want to delete.

2. Open the Table menu, click on Delete, and choose Row/ Column. Freelance opens the Delete Column/Row dialog box.

3. Choose Row or Column.

4. Click OK, and Freelance removes the highlighted row or column from the chart.

MOVING COLUMNS AND ROWS

Not only can you add and delete rows and columns of cells, you can rearrange them as well. To move a row or column, follow these steps:

1. Select the column or row you want to move by dragging the pointer across it.

2. Open the Table menu and choose Move Column/Row to open the Move Column/Row dialog box.

3. Select Column or Row to tell Freelance which you want to move.

4. Choose Before currently selected column/row to move the selected column or row to the left or up. (Choose After currently selected column/row to move the selected column or row to the right or down.)

5. Click OK. Freelance moves the selected column or row one step in the direction you indicated.

CHANGING THE STYLE OF A TABLE

Freelance's chart formatting options give you considerable control over the appearance of the tables you create. You can apply chart formatting to the entire table or to selected cells. To apply formatting to the entire table, follow these steps:

1. Right-click on the table and choose Table Properties from the shortcut menu that appears. Freelance opens the Properties for Table InfoBox.

2. Click on any InfoBox tab and adjust the formatting options as needed. Table 21.1 tells what each of the tabs is used for.

3. When you finish changing formatting options, Freelance applies the settings to the entire chart.

TABLE 21.1   TABS IN THE PROPERTIES FOR TABLEINFOBOX

TAB	CONTAINS OPTIONS FOR FORMATTING...
Text	Font, size, style, and color for all text in the table
Alignment	Alignment and indents
Bullets	Bullet size, style, and position
Line & Fill	Cell borders and backgrounds—color and style
Row/Column	Height/width of cells

TAB	CONTAINS OPTIONS FOR FORMATTING...
Layout	The table itself (the same options you choose from when you create the table)
Screen Show	Screen show settings

FORMATTING THE CONTENTS OF A CELL

In addition to overall table formatting, you can apply formatting to individual selected cells by following these steps:

1. Right-click on the table and choose Cell Properties from the shortcut menu. Freelance opens the Properties for Selected Cell(s) InfoBox.

2. Drag the pointer across the cells you want to change to highlight them.

3. Click on the tabs in the InfoBox and adjust the settings as needed. Table 21.2 describes the available tabs.

4. When you finish changing the formatting options, Freelance applies the formatting to the selected cells, overriding the general table formatting.

TABLE 21.2   TABS IN THE PROPERTIES FOR SELECTED CELLS INFOBOX

TAB	CONTAINS OPTIONS FOR FORMATTING...
Text	Font, size, style, and color for all text in the table
Alignment	Alignment and indents
Bullets	Bullet size, style, and position
Line & Fill	Cell borders and backgrounds (color and style)

In this lesson, you learned how to create and format tables. In the next lesson, you'll learn how to add art to your presentation pages.

Adding Art to Your Pages

*In this lesson, you'll learn to use the drawing tools
to draw lines, arrows, rectangles, circles, curves, and more.
You will also learn how to add clip art images to your pages.*

Introducing the Drawing Tools

For those times when none of the standard page layouts, charts, diagrams, and clip art are quite right, Freelance offers a full set of drawing tools that you can use to create drawings of your own. Using the drawing tools (available only in Current Page view), you can create basic shapes, which you can then combine to produce the logos, drawings, maps, and illustrations you need.

Freelance keeps the drawing tools out of sight until you need them. To use the drawing tools, you first open the Drawing & Text tool palette using either of two methods:

- Click on the Drawing & Text button.

- Open the Create menu, choose Drawing/Diagram and select the Make Your Own option.

The Drawing & Text tool palette appears, as shown in Figure 22.1. The palette stays on-screen until you close it by clicking on Close (X) in the upper-right corner of the palette.

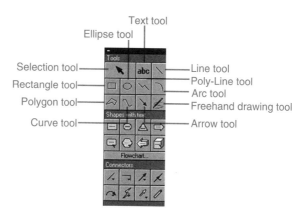

FIGURE 22.1   The Drawing & Text tool palette contains Freelance's drawing tools.

DRAWING LINES AND ARROWS

Perhaps the simplest objects to draw are the straight lines and arrows. Simply follow these steps:

1. Click on the Line or Arrow tool. The pointer changes to a cross hair.

2. Click on the starting point for the line.

3. Click on the ending point for the line. Freelance draws a straight line connecting the two points. If you chose the arrow tool, there's an arrowhead at the line's ending point.

DRAWING ARCS

Drawing arcs is easy once you get the hang of it, but it may seem strange at first. Just remember that it takes three points to define an arc: two endpoints and a midpoint. Follow these steps to draw an arc:

1. Click on the Arc tool.

2. Click on the starting point for the arc.

3. Click on the endpoint for the arc. Freelance draws a straight dotted line between the two points.

4. Click on the midpoint for the arc, and Freelance draws the arc immediately. The midpoint doesn't have to be the exact middle of the arc; even if it's off to one side, Freelance automatically draws the arc so that it starts at the starting point, passes through the midpoint, and ends at the ending point.

Preview the Arc If you click and hold down the mouse button when you place the midpoint, Freelance draws the arc as a dotted line. As long as you continue to hold down the mouse button, you can drag the pointer and watch the arc change to reflect the changing midpoint position. Release the mouse button to finalize the arc.

DRAWING RECTANGLES AND ELLIPSES

Although rectangles and ellipses seem quite different, you use the same technique to draw the objects. The only difference is which tool you choose. To draw a rectangle or ellipse, follow these steps:

1. Click on the Rectangle or Ellipse tool. The pointer changes to a cross hair.

2. Click where you want to place one corner of the rectangle, hold down the mouse button, and drag the pointer toward the opposite corner. As you drag, a dotted rectangle appears, showing the size and shape of the rectangle you're creating. (In the case of an ellipse, you're drawing an imaginary rectangle that defines the height and width of the ellipse.)

3. When the dotted rectangle is the correct size and shape, release the mouse button to drop the opposite corner. Freelance draws the rectangle or ellipse using default border and fill settings. You can change those properties and others later.

 TIP **Squares and Circles**   Creating a perfect square or circle isn't difficult in Freelance. If you hold down the Shift key as you drag to create a rectangle or ellipse, Freelance forces the height and width to always remain equal.

DRAWING POLYGONS AND POLY-LINES

Polygons and poly-lines are both composed of multiple straight line segments. The difference between them is that polygons are enclosed shapes that can have a fill color and pattern, while poly-lines are open-ended lines.

To create a polygon or poly-line object, follow these steps:

1. Click on the Polygon or Poly-Line tool.

2. Click to place the starting point of the first line segment.

3. Click to position the ending point for the first line segment. Freelance draws a dotted line connecting the two points. Because polygons and poly-lines are composed of multiple segments, the endpoint for one line segment is also the starting point for the next line segment. Therefore, the tool remains selected so you can add more points to create additional line segments.

4. Click to position the endpoint for the next line segment. Freelance draws the line segment with a dotted line.

5. Continue adding points to define line segments as necessary.

6. Click on the Select tool to deactivate the Polygon or Poly-Line tool and complete the object. Freelance converts the temporary dotted line segments to real lines. If you've created a polygon, Freelance automatically closes the shape by connecting the end of the last line segment to the starting point of the first line segment.

DRAWING CURVES

Drawing a curve is essentially the same as drawing a poly-line. However, when you finish drawing, Freelance goes back and arches the line segments so that the resulting line curves through the connecting points between line segments instead of connecting at sharp angles. Later, you can go back and edit the curve in Points Mode (see Lesson 23) to change the shape of the curve.

To create a curve, simply follow the steps for creating a poly-line.

 TIP **Preview the Curve** When drawing a curve, start with the pointer a short distance from the previous point, press and hold the mouse button, and drag the mouse. Freelance draws a dotted preview line as soon as you press the mouse button so you can watch the curve change as you drag. Release the mouse button when you're satisfied with the location of the endpoint and the shape of the curve.

DRAWING FREEHAND LINES

The Freehand tool is perhaps the most intuitive of the drawing tools. However, many people find it difficult to use because it is awkward to "draw" with a mouse.

To draw freehand lines, follow these steps:

1. Click on the Freehand tool.

2. Move the cross-hair pointer to the location where you want to start the freehand line.

3. Press and hold the mouse button and drag the mouse. Freelance creates a freeform line tracing the path of the mouse pointer.

4. Release the mouse button to finish the line.

ADDING CLIP ART TO A PAGE

Adding clip art images to your presentation pages adds visual interest. Freelance comes with an assortment of clip art drawings and an easy-to-use clip art library. You can add any of those clip art images to your page.

To add clip art from the clip art library to a presentation page, follow these steps:

1. Select the page to which you want to add the clip art and switch to Current Page view if necessary.

2. Click on the Clip Art button, or open the Create menu and choose Add Clip Art. The Add Clip Art or Diagram to the Page Dialog box (shown in Figure 22.2) appears.

 TIP **Click Here to Add Clip Art** If you create a new page using the Bullets & Clip Art layout, you can click on the Click here placeholder to open the Clip Art Library. From there, continue with step 3 to add clip art to your page.

3. Pick a category from the drop-down list.

4. Use the left and right arrows next to the Scan button to scroll through the clip art images in the selected category.

5. Click on the thumbnail of the clip art image you want to add to your page.

Select a category here.

Thumbnails of the
clip art images

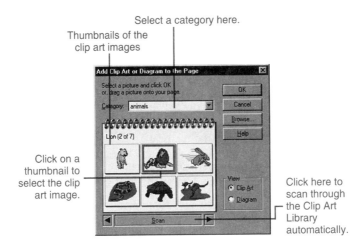

Click on a
thumbnail to
select the clip
art image.

Click here to
scan through
the Clip Art
Library
automatically.

FIGURE 22.2 The Add Clip Art or Diagram to the Page dialog
box.

6. Click OK to close the dialog box. Freelance adds the clip
art drawing to your page. The clip art drawing is selected,
which means you can move, resize, or edit it as you
would any other object.

ADDING A BITMAP TO A PAGE

You're not limited to using only the images in the clip art library.
You can also add bitmaps to your presentation pages in Current
Page view.

Bitmap A *bitmap* (also called a *raster* or *paint* image) is
composed of rows and rows of tiny colored dots. Scan-
ners and programs such as Paint and Photoshop create
bitmap images.

Follow these steps to add a bitmap to your page:

1. Open the Create menu and choose Add Bitmap. Freelance displays the Add a Bitmap dialog box.

2. In the Files of type list, choose the correct file type for the file you want to use. The default file type is Windows/PM Bitmap (BMP), but you can use other common bitmap file types such as TIF and PCX.

3. Change to a different drive or folder in the Look in box if necessary, and then click on the file you want to bring into Freelance.

4. Click on the Open button. Freelance imports the bitmap file and places the image on your page. You can select, move, and resize the bitmap as you would any other object.

Before Freelance imports the image, you may see another dialog box asking whether you want to place a copy of the bitmap in the Freelance presentation. Normally, you should answer Yes to store a duplicate copy of the bitmap within your Freelance presentation file. The alternative is to store a *link* to the original bitmap file on your disk. When you store a link, Freelance simply refers to the bitmap file whenever it needs to. This saves disk space and reduces the size of your presentation file. However, if you move the bitmap file, Freelance will not be able to locate it the next time you open your presentation.

In this lesson, you learned how to use the tools in the Drawing & Text tool palette to create basic lines and shapes. You also learned how to add clip art and bitmap images to your pages. In the next lesson, you'll learn some more advanced drawing techniques.

More Drawing Techniques

*In this lesson, you'll expand your Freelance drawing
skills by learning how to combine and convert object
types, reshape objects, and use drawing grids and rulers.*

Drawing Lines with Both Straight and Curved Sections

In the previous lesson, you learned to use the Poly-Line and
Curve tools to draw lines with straight segments and lines with
curves. But you may need to draw a line with both straight and
curved sections. Freelance gives you a couple of ways to do this.
You can combine the creation processes as you create the line you
need, or you can draw each of the lines separately and then combine them into one.

To draw a line that is part poly-line and part curve, follow these
steps:

1. Click on the Poly-Line tool.

2. Click to add points to define straight line segments as
   necessary (see Lesson 22). When you finish the straight-
   line section, do *not* click on the Select tool to finish the
   object.

3. Click on the Curve tool.

4. Click to add more points to the line, defining the curved
   segments.

5. Switch back and forth between straight and curved sections as necessary by clicking on the Poly-Line and Curve tools.

6. When you finish drawing the line, click on the Selection tool to deselect the other tools and finalize the line.

To combine two separate lines into a single object that contains both straight and curved sections, first create the lines. Then follow these steps to connect the two lines:

1. Select both lines by clicking on one, pressing and holding down the Shift key, and clicking on the other. (Do not select the lines by dragging a marquee selection box around them.)

2. Open the Drawing menu and choose Connect Lines. Freelance combines the two lines into one, drawing a new line segment to connect them.

CHANGING AN OBJECT'S TYPE

Freelance enables you to change lines (poly-lines, freehand lines, or curves) to polygons and change polygons, rectangles, and ellipses to lines. You simply select a command from a shortcut menu to tell Freelance what kind of change you want to make.

To change a line to a polygon, for example, you first select the line. (It can't be a straight line.) Then right-click on the line, point to Convert, and click on To Polygons from the shortcut menu. Freelance adds a line segment to close the shape and converts the line to a polygon.

You can use the same technique to convert a polygon, rectangle, or ellipse to a line. When you right-click on a polygon, the shortcut menu includes the Convert command and the To Lines command.

EDITING POINTS

If every object you draw is perfectly shaped on the first try, you can skip this section. It's more likely, though, that you sometimes have to reshape the lines, arcs, curves, and polygons you draw. If so, Points Mode is for you.

To switch to Points Mode to edit lines and polygons, open the Edit menu and choose Points Mode, or press Shift+F6. The pointer changes to an arrow with a small "o" inside to indicate that you are in Points Mode.

 You can repeat the command to toggle Points Mode off again, but you may not need to. When you work in Points Mode, the pointer performs most of its normal functions, and you can edit drawn objects point-by-point.

SELECTING, DELETING, AND MOVING POINTS

In Points Mode, Freelance enables you to edit the individual points that define the shape of lines, poly-lines, arcs, curves, polygons, arrows, and freehand lines. You can't edit the points in rectangles and circles unless you convert them to lines first.

To select the points you want to edit, follow these steps:

1. Click on the object you want to edit. Instead of the usual selection handles, smaller hollow-box handles appear on each of the points that define the object.

2. Click on the point you want to manipulate. Freelance fills in the hollow selection handle on that point (see Figure 23.1) to indicate that the particular point is selected.

 Selecting Multiple Points   To select more than one point at the same time, select the first point, press and hold the Shift key, and select any additional points.

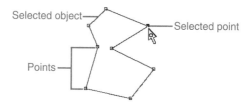

FIGURE 23.1   Select the points you want to edit in Points Mode.

You can delete a selected point using either of these methods:

- Open the Edit menu, choose Edit Points, and then choose Delete Points.

- Simply press the Delete key.

Freelance immediately redraws the object without that point.

To reshape an object by moving points, follow these steps:

1. Select the point (or points) you want to move.

2. Click and drag the selected point. As you drag, Freelance displays a dotted line showing the object's new shape.

3. When the shape's size looks right, release the mouse button to drop the point at its new location.

ADDING POINTS

To add points to an object, follow these steps:

1. Open the Edit menu, choose Edit Points, and then choose Add Point. The pointer changes to an arrow containing a plus sign.

2. If the object to which you want to add a point isn't already selected, click on it to select it.

3. Click on the line segment or polygon side where you want to add the point. Freelance adds a new point at that location, and the pointer loses its plus sign.

4. Drag the new point to reshape the line or polygon. (That's why you added the point isn't it?)

RESHAPING CURVES

Reshaping curves is a bit different from reshaping other object types. Curves have extra handles at each point to define the sweep or shape of the curve.

When you select a point on a curve, the extra handles appear, connected to the main point by dotted lines (see Figure 23.2). Notice that the curve goes through the main point, but not the extra handles.

FIGURE 23.2   Each point on a curve has extra handles with which you can reshape the curve.

Move the main point to reshape the curve just as you would move a point to reshape a poly-line. In addition, you can move the extra handles beside the point to reshape the curve. The extra handles act like magnets, influencing the curve without necessarily touching it. Using the points and handles to shape curves takes some getting used to. The best way to learn is to try it.

PRECISION DRAWING WITH GRIDS AND THE RULER

Freelance includes an on-screen ruler to help you size and position the objects you draw. To turn the ruler display on or off, open the View menu and choose Show Ruler.

Another drawing aid is the grid. To use the grid, follow these steps:

1. Open the View menu and choose Set Units & Grid. The Set Units & Grid dialog box shown in Figure 23.3 appears.

FIGURE 23.3   Adjust the grid settings from this dialog box.

2. Change the following settings to your liking:

   Units   Click on the option button for the unit of measure for the ruler and grid.

   Display grid   Check this box to display the grid as dots on your screen.

   Snap to grid   Check this box to force objects and points to jump to the nearest grid point.

   Horizontal space/Vertical space   Specify the horizontal and vertical grid spacing.

3. When you finish making your choices, click OK to close the dialog box and put your grid choices into effect.

In this lesson, you learned how to connect lines, convert lines to polygons and vice versa, edit points to reshape objects, and use the drawing grid and the ruler. In the next lesson, you'll learn how to group, arrange, and manipulate the objects you draw.

GROUPING, ARRANGING, AND MANIPULATING OBJECTS

In this lesson, you'll learn how to define groups of objects, how to manipulate objects, and how to create curved text effects.

GROUPING AND UNGROUPING OBJECTS

Freelance enables you to combine objects into groups that you can then select and manipulate as a single unit. Later, you can reverse the process and dissolve the group if you need to edit individual objects. To create a group, follow these steps:

1. Select the objects you want to combine into a group. (Select objects by holding down the Shift key and clicking on each object or by using any of the other selection techniques covered in Lesson 12.)

2. Right-click on the selected objects and choose Group from the shortcut menu. The individual selection handles around each object are replaced by one set of selection handles around the group. You can now select and manipulate the group as if it were a single object.

To dissolve the group so you can access and work with the individual component objects, follow these steps:

1. Select the group.

2. Right-click on the group and choose Ungroup from the shortcut menu (or open the Group menu and choose Ungroup). The group reverts to a collection of individual objects.

ALIGNING OBJECTS

When you need to align objects in your drawing, you can let Freelance help get them aligned accurately. To align objects, follow these steps:

1. Select the objects.

2. Right-click on one of the selected objects and choose Align from the shortcut menu (or open the Drawing menu and choose Align). The Align Objects dialog box shown in Figure 24.1 appears.

FIGURE 24.1   You can align one object or several.

3. Select the alignment type you want and click OK. Freelance aligns the selected objects as you specified.

FLIPPING OBJECTS

You can flip an object or group to create a mirror image of the original. To do so, follow these steps:

1. Select the object or group you want to flip.

2. Open the Drawing menu and choose Flip.

3. Choose Left-Right or Top-Bottom from the flyout menu. Freelance flips the object (or group) instantly.

ROTATING OBJECTS

Another helpful object manipulation command enables you to
rotate an object (or group) around its center. The following steps
teach you how to rotate an object:

1. Select the object you want to rotate.

2. Right-click on the object and choose Rotate from the
   shortcut menu. The pointer changes to a plus sign and
   an arched arrow.

3. Drag in a circle around the object. A dotted rectangle
   representing the object rotates to follow the pointer.

4. Release the mouse button to drop the rectangle at its new
   angle. Freelance redraws the object, rotated to a new
   angle.

Controlling Rotation Angles   When rotating an object,
TIP   you can hold down the Shift key as you drag to rotate in
45-degree increments.

OVERLAPPING OBJECTS

Freelance draws objects on the screen one at a time in the order in
which you create them. The objects can overlap; however, if they
do, the objects that you've drawn most recently will partially (or
completely) obscure the objects that you drew earlier. You can
change the order, or priority, of the objects on the page to change
which object appears in front. (It's a bit like shuffling a deck of
cards.)

To change the order in which Freelance draws objects, follow these steps:

1. Select the object you want to place in front of or behind other objects.

2. Right-click on the object and choose Priority from the shortcut menu.

3. From the flyout menu, select one of the following options:

> **Bring to Front**   Moves the selected object to the top of the stack.
>
> **Send to Back**   Moves the selected object to the bottom of the stack.
>
> **Bring Forward One**   Moves the selected object one level closer to the top of the stack.
>
> **Send Back One**   Moves the selected object one level closer to the bottom of the stack.

 Stacking the Deck   You may need to repeat the process a few times to get the object properly positioned in front of some objects and behind others.

CHANGING OBJECT PROPERTIES

All objects have colors and other formatting attributes, just as text does. Freelance provides the InfoBox as a standard way for you to control those attributes for any object.

To change the color of an object or adjust other properties, follow these steps:

1. Select the object.

2. Right-click on the object and choose (Object Type) Properties from the shortcut menu. Freelance displays the

InfoBox, showing the properties for the selected object type. (The tabs and settings that appear in the InfoBox vary depending on what kind of object you're working with.)

3. Adjust the settings as necessary.

4. Click on the Close (X) button to close the InfoBox.

Not only can you change object properties with the InfoBox, you can also copy attributes from one object to another with Fast Formats. Pick up the attributes of one object and apply them to others just as you do with text objects. Lesson 16 covers the Fast Formats feature in detail.

Where's the Command? If the Fast Formats command doesn't appear on the shortcut menu when you right-click on an object, see if it's available on the Drawing, Collection, Text, or Text Shape menus.

CURVING TEXT

Freelance reserves one type of object manipulation just for text objects. You can curve text to follow a predefined path, which creates some impressive special effects. To curve text in your presentation, follow these steps:

1. Create and select the text object.

2. Open the Text menu and choose Curved text. Freelance opens the Curved Text dialog box, shown in Figure 24.2.

3. Scroll through the list as necessary and click on the text shape you want to use.

4. If you chose a full-circle effect, enter a number in the Text start point box.

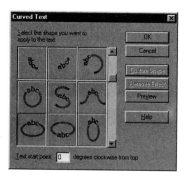

FIGURE 24.2   Choose a text effect from the Curved Text dialog box.

5. Click on the Preview button to see what your text will look like.

6. If you like the effect, click OK. If you don't, click on the Change button to return to the Curved Text dialog box and make another selection. Then repeat steps 5 and 6.

If you decide later that you don't like the curved text effect, you can select the text object, reopen the Curved Text dialog box, and click on the Remove Effect button to return the text to normal.

In this lesson, you learned how to define groups of objects, use several object manipulation tools, change object properties, and create curved text effects. In the next lesson, you'll learn how to create speaker notes and handouts to supplement your presentation.

CREATING NOTES AND HANDOUTS

In this lesson, you'll learn how to create speaker notes and audience handouts from your presentation pages.

SPEAKER NOTES

Freelance enables you to create speaker notes on a separate page of text linked to a presentation page. Typically, you use speaker notes to store the notes you make about your presentation, but you might also use them to store supplementary information about the presentation page or even the script for your speech.

Normally, speaker notes are hidden from view. But when you need them, you can display speaker notes in a special window in Current Page, Page Sorter, or Outliner views and in Rehearse mode (which you'll learn about in Lesson 26). And as you will see in Lesson 27, with Freelance's printing options, you can print speaker notes on the same page with your presentation pages.

CREATING SPEAKER NOTES

To create a speaker note for a presentation page, follow these steps:

1. Open the Page menu and choose Create Speaker Note. Freelance opens the Speaker Note window, shown in Figure 25.1.

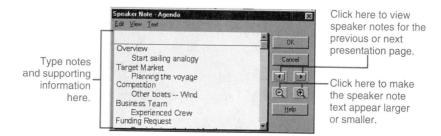

Type notes and supporting information here.

Click here to view speaker notes for the previous or next presentation page.

Click here to make the speaker note text appear larger or smaller.

Figure 25.1   Freelance's special window for speaker notes.

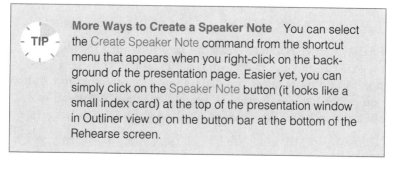

More Ways to Create a Speaker Note   You can select the Create Speaker Note command from the shortcut menu that appears when you right-click on the background of the presentation page. Easier yet, you can simply click on the Speaker Note button (it looks like a small index card) at the top of the presentation window in Outliner view or on the button bar at the bottom of the Rehearse screen.

2. Type the text of your note.

3. Click OK to close the Speaker Note window. Freelance saves the speaker note in your presentation file and places a Speaker Note icon above the page's thumbnail in Outliner view (see Figure 25.2). A similar icon appears beneath the page thumbnail in Page Sorter view.

Once you create a speaker note for a presentation page, you can view it using any of the following techniques:

- Open the Page menu and choose Open Speaker Note.

- In Outliner view, select the page and click on the Speaker Note button at the top of the presentation window.

- Click on the small Speaker Note icon that appears beside the page thumbnail in Outliner or Page Sorter view.

- In Rehearse mode, click on the Speaker Note button on the button bar at the bottom of the screen.

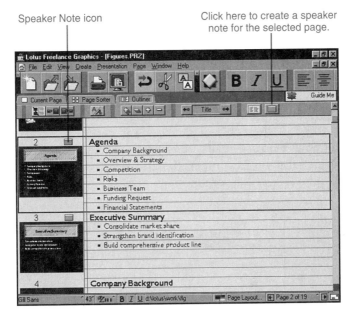

FIGURE 25.2   Freelance places an icon beside the thumbnails of pages with speaker notes attached.

The speaker note for the current (or selected) page appears in a special window on top of the presentation window. As long as the speaker note window is open, you can view, edit, or add to the text of the note.

FORMATTING TEXT IN SPEAKER NOTES

You can change the appearance of the text in your speaker notes by following these steps:

1. Open the Speaker Note window.

2. Select the text you want to format.

3. Open the Speaker Note window's Text menu and choose Text Properties. Freelance displays the Text Properties for Speaker Notes dialog box.

4. Adjust the settings as necessary. To make your changes affect all the text in all Speaker Notes in the presentation, check the Apply to all speaker notes check box.

5. Click OK to close the dialog box and apply the formatting to your speaker note text.

Printing Speaker Notes

When you print your presentation, you can choose to print speaker notes alongside your presentation pages (as shown in Figure 25.3). Lesson 27 contains the instructions you need for setting printing options for your presentation.

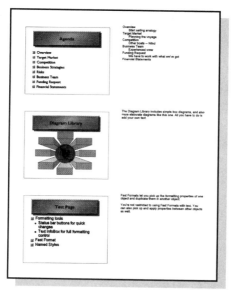

Figure 25.3　Print your presentation page and speaker notes on the same page for easy reference.

SPEAKING FROM AN OUTLINE

Many presenters like to speak from an outline. Consequently, Freelance offers you the option of printing the outline you see on-screen in Outliner view. To print your presentation outline, follow these steps.

1. Switch to Outliner view.

2. Open the File menu and choose Print. The Print dialog box appears.

3. In the Print area in the lower-left portion of the dialog box, choose Outline.

4. (Optional) Adjust other dialog box settings, options, and page setup as necessary. (You'll learn more about printing options in Lesson 27.)

5. When you finish making changes, click on the Print button. Freelance prints your presentation as an outline (without page thumbnails).

HANDOUTS AND AUDIENCE NOTES

Handouts are simply printouts of your presentation pages. Providing your audience with handouts makes your presentation more effective because the audience can refer to your key points or the data you present.

Freelance also makes it easy to prepare and print *audience notes*. Audience notes are similar to handouts, but they are formatted with space beside each presentation page so the audience members can take their own notes.

Both handouts and audience notes are part of the standard options available when you print your presentation. Again, see Lesson 27 for more on printing and the printing options.

In this lesson, you learned how to create speaker notes and audience handouts from your presentation. In the next lesson, you'll learn how to create a screen show of your presentation.

SETTING UP A SCREEN SHOW

In this lesson, you'll learn how to play your presentation as a screen show, how to set up basic transitions and effects, and how to use the rehearse mode.

VIEWING A PRESENTATION AS A SCREEN SHOW

A screen show displays your presentation pages full-screen, without the distractions of windows, menus, and SmartIcons. But a screen show can be more than just a display of static presentation pages. You can create transitions and multimedia effects that turn your presentation into a cinematic production.

Screen Show A screen show displays your presentation pages full-screen, one after the other, in sequence. A screen show can include transition effects between pages, bullet builds, sounds, movies, and other effects.

To run your presentation as a screen show, follow these steps:

1. Open the Presentation menu, choose Run Screen Show, and choose From Beginning (or From Current Page).

2. Freelance draws the first page of your presentation full-screen, covering all windows and desktop elements that are currently on your screen.

3. To advance to the next page of the screen show, click the mouse button (or press the Page Down key or Enter).

What About My Other Windows?   If you need to start or switch to another program, press Ctrl+Esc to display the Windows 95 taskbar, and then click on any of the open programs' taskbar buttons or open the Start menu.

4. When you reach the end of the presentation, the screen show ends automatically, and the normal Freelance window reappears on your screen. If you need to exit the screen show early, press Esc and click on Quit Screen Show in the dialog box that appears.

SETTING SCREEN SHOW OPTIONS

Freelance provides a lot of choices for controlling transitions, timing, and options for your screen shows. Some settings affect the screen show as a whole, some affect individual pages, and some affect specific objects.

To set up your basic screen show options, follow these steps:

1. Pull down the Presentation menu and choose Set Up Screen Show. Freelance opens the Set Up Screen Show dialog box shown in Figure 26.1.

2. Click on the Page Effects tab if necessary. The options on this tab establish the default transition and timing for your presentation screen show. (You can change these settings for individual pages.)

> **Apply to**   Choose which pages you want the transition to apply to (all existing pages or new pages only).
>
> **Transition**   Choose a page transition from the list.
>
> **Display next page**   By default, the screen show advances only when you click the mouse button or press a key. Alternatively, you can set it up to run automatically, advancing to the next page after a specified pause.

FIGURE 26.1   The Set Up Screen Show dialog box with the Page Effects tab showing.

3. Click on the Tools tab. Figure 26.2 shows the Tools tab.

FIGURE 26.2   Configure your on-screen toolbox with these options.

4. Choose which of the following screen show tools you want to use:

Control panel   Click on the Display control panel check box to display a set of VCR-style buttons you can use to navigate your screen show. If you choose to use the control panel, open the Position drop-down list and indicate which corner of the screen you want the control panel to appear in.

On-screen drawing   Check this option if you want to be able to draw on-screen with the mouse during your screen show. If you activate this option, select a color and line width for the lines you draw.

5. Click on the Options tab to access the screen show options shown in Figure 26.3 and described here.

Cue for displaying next page   If you want Freelance to tell you when it finishes drawing one page and is ready to advance to the next, indicate whether you want it to alert you with a sound or a small arrow in the corner of the screen.

Run Options   Check Start screen show automatically when file is opened to have Freelance run the screen show immediately whenever you open the presentation file. Check the Run screen show in a continuous loop option if you want the screen show to start over automatically when it finishes.

Overrides   Although you may have established different settings for individual pages, this option lets you override those settings and run the screen show with automatic page advance. You don't have to change the settings for each page, and you can reinstate the individual page settings simply by deselecting this option.

6. When you finish adjusting the settings, click OK to close the Set Up Screen Show dialog box. The settings take effect the next time you run the screen show.

FIGURE 26.3   The Options tab of the Set Up Screen Show dialog box.

How Do I Make It Stop?!   To stop a screen show running in a loop, press Esc and choose Exit Screen Show from the dialog box that appears.

CREATING PAGE EFFECTS AND TRANSITIONS

In the Set Up Screen Show dialog box, you can establish page transitions and timings for the entire presentation. But you can add variety by setting the transition effects and timing for each page individually. Follow these steps to set the transition and timing for an individual presentation page.

1. Go to or select the page.

2. Right-click on the page and choose Page Properties from the shortcut menu. Freelance opens the Properties for Page InfoBox.

3. Click on the Screen Show tab (its icon looks like a movie projector).

4. Adjust the following settings to reflect how you want this particular page to appear in the screen show:

> **Transition** Select a transition effect from the list.
>
> **Sound** Specify a sound to play when the page appears. Use the Browse button to help you locate the sound file.
>
> **Advance to next page** Choose Trigger manually if you want to advance the presentation page by page, or choose Trigger automatically and specify how long you want this page to remain on-screen.
>
> **Do not display this page during screen show** Check this box to skip this page during your screen show.

5. Click on the Close (X) button to close the InfoBox. The settings take effect the next time you run the screen show.

CREATING BULLET BUILDS

An effective presentation technique is to *build* or display a bulleted list one bullet at a time. Freelance includes a feature that makes this task easy. To set up a bulleted list build, follow these steps:

1. Go to or select the page containing the text block you want to show as a bullet build.

2. Select the text block.

3. Right-click on the text block and choose Text Properties from the shortcut menu. Freelance opens the Properties for All Text Levels InfoBox.

4. Click on the Screen Show tab to display the options shown in Figure 26.4.

Figure 26.4   Set up a bullet build in your screen show.

5. In the Timing area, choose Display page first, then display text. Then choose whether you want Freelance to display the next text block at your command (when you click) or automatically after a specified number of seconds.

6. Open the Display bullets drop-down list and select One at a time to make the bullets appear one at a time.

7. Open the Transition drop-down list and choose the transition you want Freelance to use as it displays each bullet. If you want Freelance to dim the color of the existing bullet before displaying a new one, check the Dim previous bullets option.

8. Open the Sound drop-down list and specify a sound for Freelance to play when each bullet appears. Click the Options button to access controls for when and how many times the sound plays.

9. When you finish setting the options, click on the Close (X) button to close the InfoBox. Then run the screen show to see the effect of your bullet build.

REHEARSING A PRESENTATION

One key to feeling confident and comfortable when making a presentation is to practice, practice, practice. To help you practice your presentation, Freelance includes a special rehearse mode. Using rehearse mode is similar to running a screen show, but it adds some special on-screen buttons and timers to keep you apprised of the time you spend on each page and the total time for the presentation.

To rehearse a presentation, pull down the Presentation menu, click on Rehearse, and choose Start. Freelance displays the first page of the presentation full-screen and adds a control panel of buttons across the botton of the screen as shown in Figure 26.5.

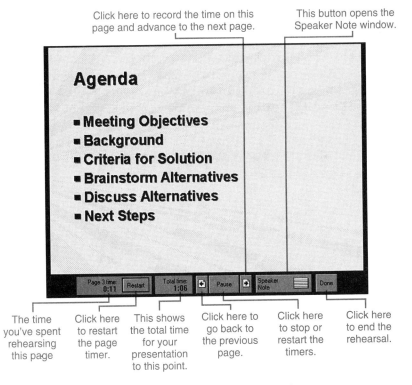

FIGURE 26.5 You can rehearse your presentation.

Not Your First?   If you've already rehearsed the presentation, Freelance opens a Warning dialog box before starting the rehearsal. In the dialog box, you choose whether to keep the page timings from the previous rehearsal or replace them with the times you record in the new rehearsal.

During the rehearsal, use the rehearse mode buttons to step through the presentation page by page. As you do, Freelance keeps track of how long you spend on each page and how long you spend on the presentation as a whole. If you flub up on a page, you don't have to start over from the beginning. Just click the Restart button to reset the timers to the beginning of the current page. Other buttons let you pause and restart the timers and refer to (or create) Speaker Notes.

When you finish the rehearsal, Freelance displays the Rehearse Summary dialog box shown in Figure 26.6. Here you can review the page timings to check the pace of your presentation. Click OK to close the dialog box and return to the regular Freelance application window.

Rehearse Summary		
Page	Time	Total
1. Opening	0:22	0:22
2. The Problem	0:32	0:54
3. Agenda	0:29	1:23
4. 18.6	0:33	1:56
5. 22.2	0:36	2:32
6. 22.1	0:25	2:57
7. 18.5	0:47	3:44
8. 18.4	0:12	3:56
9. Meeting Objectives	0:38	4:34
10. Background	0:56	5:30
11. Criteria for Solutions	0:19	5:49
12. Brainstorm Now!	0:33	6:22
13. Possible Solutions	0:43	7:05

Total presentation time: 8:21   OK   Help

FIGURE 26.6   Compare your page timings to check the pace of your presentation.

In this lesson, you learned how to play your presentation as a screen show and how to set up basic transitions and effects for a screen show. In the next lesson, you'll learn how to print your presentation.

PRINTING YOUR PRESENTATION

In this lesson, you'll learn how to print your presentation and explore some of Freelance's printing options.

When you finish your presentation, you may want to print all or parts of it. Freelance provides you with lots of options so you can control exactly what and how you print. Because there are so many options, I'm going to give you the bare-bones instructions on how to print in this first section. However, the rest of the lesson is devoted to helping you understand the various options and settings.

WHEN YOU'RE READY TO PRINT...

To print your presentation, follow these basic steps:

1. Open the File menu and choose Print. Freelance opens the Print dialog box shown in Figure 27.1.

2. Adjust settings and choose options according to your preferences.

3. Click on the Print button to begin printing your presentation.

SELECTING A PRINTER

Use the controls in the Printer section of the dialog box to tell Freelance about the printer you want to use. The Print to list box shows your default Windows printer unless you select a different printer from the drop-down list. You can select any printer (or printer driver) you have installed in Windows.

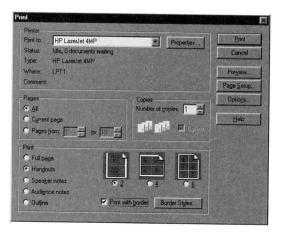

FIGURE 27.1   The Print dialog box contains Freelance's printing options.

When you select a different printer, Freelance immediately goes through your presentation and checks each page to make sure all your text, charts, and drawings fit within the printer's printable area. If Freelance finds a problem, it displays the Device/Paper Size Mismatch dialog box. Choose whether you want to ignore the problem (you can fix it manually before you print) or whether you want Freelance to automatically scale down everything on the problem page to fit within the printable area. Then click OK to return to the Print dialog box.

If you need to adjust printer-specific settings, click on the Properties button. Freelance opens the standard Windows 95 Properties dialog box for the selected printer. Adjust any necessary settings and click OK to return to the Print dialog box.

INDICATING WHICH PAGES TO PRINT

In the Pages section of the Print dialog box, you specify which pages you want to print. You can choose to print all pages or the current page only, or you can specify a range of page numbers.

Printing Non-Contiguous Pages   To print certain pages that do not fall in a contiguous block, go to Page Sorter view and select the pages you want to print by clicking on the first page, holding down the Shift key, and clicking on all other pages. Then open the Print dialog box and choose Pages selected in sorter in the Pages section.

In the Copies area, specify how many copies of each page you want to print and whether you want those copies collated into sets automatically.

Setting Up the Page

You can click on the Page Setup button in the Print dialog box (or pull down the File menu and choose Page Setup) to open the Page Setup dialog box shown in Figure 27.2. Use the options in this dialog box to create headers and footers and to select page orientation for your presentation pages.

- **Headers & Footers**   Define *headers and footers* (text that prints at the top and bottom of every page) by typing information into the text boxes. You can insert fields for the page number, current date, current time, and presentation file name by clicking on the appropriate buttons. Freelance adds the field at the cursor position and inserts the corresponding information when you print.

- **Orientation**   The orientation setting controls the orientation of your presentation pages—not of the printed pages. Choose Portrait or Landscape (there is an example of each one next to its option button).

When you finish making your page setup choices, click OK to close the dialog box.

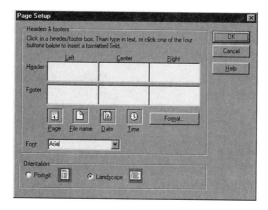

FIGURE 27.2   Define headers and footers in the Page Setup dialog box.

 TIP   **SmartMaster Looks Like Landscape**   Most SmartMaster looks are designed for landscape orientation and may not work well in portrait orientation. Landscape orientation is preferred (and sometimes required) for screen shows, 35mm slides, and overheads.

USING PRINTING OPTIONS

Click on the Options button to open the Options dialog box. You can select any combination of options in this dialog box.

Adjust output library for printing   By default, Freelance automatically adjusts its color library to optimize the color output for any one of several popular color printers. It has no effect with other printers.

Print graduated fills as solid   Select this option to allow faster printing and to solve printer memory problems that result from trying to print complex graduated fills.

Print with blank background (no look)   You might want to select this option to speed printing or to simplify the printed pages by eliminating the background.

After you select your printing options, click OK to close this dialog box and return to the Print dialog box.

Selecting What to Print

Perhaps the most important settings in the Print dialog box are in the Print area; there you specify what kind of output you want from your presentation file.

Presentation Pages

Choose the Full page option to print one presentation page on each printer page. This option prints your presentation pages at the maximum size allowed by the printer. Use the Full page output option when you need the best possible quality for overheads, report pages, and the like.

Handouts and Notes

Although you can use full-page printouts as handouts for your audience, you'll probably want to print two or more presentation pages on each paper page for handouts. Choose Handouts, and then choose 2, 4, or 6 presentation pages per printed page.

Choose the Speaker notes option to print speaker notes alongside your presentation pages. Then choose 1, 2, or 3. Choosing 2 prints the presentation page at the top of the paper page with the speaker notes beneath it and so on.

Select the Audience notes option to print pages that are similar to the speaker notes pages. Audience notes show the presentation pages but leave space for the audience members to make their own notes. Again, choose 1, 2, or 3.

OUTLINE

In Lesson 25, you learned that you can print your presentation text in outline form (as it appears in Outliner view). For the Outline option to be available here, you must be in Outliner view when you open the Print dialog box.

35MM SLIDES

It's very unlikely that you have an output device attached to your computer that's capable of producing 35mm slides. However, you can produce 35mm slides of your Freelance presentation by sending them to a service bureau that specializes in slide output.

Some service bureaus will print slides from a copy of your presentation file. Others will supply a special slide output driver that you install in Windows like a printer driver. To use a slide driver, first choose the slide driver as the printer in the Print to box. Then choose the Full page option, and Freelance "prints" your presentation into a special file that you can take to a service bureau for output on its slide-making equipment.

 TIP   **Getting into Shape for Slides**   Because 35mm slides are wider than normal paper pages, it's a good idea to select the slide driver as your printer *before* you create the pages in your presentation.

Although this is the end of the *10 Minute Guide to Freelance Graphics for Windows 95*, it's not the end of the capabilities of Freelance. I've covered the basics, but you can have fun exploring its many other features on your own.

Good luck with your presentations and with Freelance Graphics for Windows 95.

INDEX

Q-R-S

T